3Stories

by
Max Robinson

Hi There…

Thanks for picking up this little book. My name is David but I write under the pen name of Max Robison, Max after my childhood pet and Robinson being the name of my maternal grandfather.

I am here bringing together three stories I wrote many years ago:

Mickey Rigg – written in 1974
Peter's Magic Fountain Pen – written in 1994
The Wild Adventures of Di Central Eating – written in 1995

Yes, I wrote these stories many years ago. Originally I used pen and paper to draft the tales then tapped them out on a typewriter. How many of you know what a typewriter is, or was ? You'll probably find one in a museum ! Across these three stories there will be things, if you are not of my generation, which will be something of an enigma to you. Have bit of fun researching what they are.

I really hope you enjoy reading these little tales but more importantly I hope they may inspire you to write something yourself. Go on. Give it a try.

Mickey Rigg

AUTHOR'S NOTE:
Way back in 1973 I was training to be a teacher. One of my college lecturers was author Dennis Hamley who had just published his first novel Pageants of Despair. He set we students an assignment to write a short story which could be read to a class of pupils in school. I wrote Mickey Rigg and had mixed emotions of pride and embarrassment when in the following tutorial Dennis Hamley read it aloud to us all. He also sent it to his publisher who responded with a note: *Sorry Dennis this is not one for us.* Disappointed yes but Dennis

encouraged me not to stop writing, mine was after all a short story and the publisher was looking for full-length books.

So here he is Mickey Rigg. Have a read of his tale.

David aka Max

Mickey Rigg was a friend of mine. As a young teenager I had lots of friends but Mickey's only friend was me. If my mother had her way Mickey Rigg would have had no friends at all, she did not approve of her only son associating with the likes of the Rigg Family

"Take no notice of her," Sis said. Older sister Janet had always looked out for me and when she gave me advice I always took it. However, I needed no advice about this friendship.

Every Saturday Mickey Rigg and I would go fishing at Powel's Pool in Sutton Park. We never caught anything, if we did I do not know what we would have done but each week we dangled worms on hooks into the water in search of the legendary Powel's Pool Pike.

My fishing rod had once belonged to my grandfather but he had died before I was born. Mickey used his father's rod, a sporting instrument of which he had no longer any use for. It cost one shilling to fish at the lake, twelve pennies my friend never had, but when the park warden came around he would issue just one permit, smile and say it covered both rods. In return Mickey always provided the worms each Saturday.

Like I say, we never caught anything. I had a keep net but all it kept was water. Catching fish, even the legendary Powel's Pool Pike was not what our Saturday mornings were about. It was the highlight of our week. Monday to Friday was school which was intrinsically boring but Saturday was fishing and that was not boring.

Mickey Rigg and I were in the same class at Boldmere High School for Boys in the Royal Borough of Sutton Coldfield but we never sat together during lessons. Seating was arranged in alphabetical order, Mickey's surname began with the letter R, mine began with a different letter. School dinners cost one shilling a day, five shillings a week. Monday morning registration included the collection of the money. In our class Mickey was the only boy who qualified for free school meals, part of Monday Morning Embarrassment was always to announce my friend's poverty.

"You know, John Boy," Sis said, "that Mickey's father is in prison and that is why he has free school dinners."

"What's he in prison for ?" I asked. I knew my friend was the son of a gangster but what crime that involved I did not know and it was something I never spoke about with Mickey.

"For breaking the law ?"

"A gangster ?"

"He is hardly Ronnie or Reggie Kray, Mr Rigg is a house burglar."

"Mickey is honest."

"I am sure he is and he is your friend you be his friend John Boy."

Mickey had an illness. He was an epileptic but I did not know what epilepsy is and could see no signs of his illness when we went fishing each Saturday. We would meet by the corner shops on Sutton Oak Road where I would spend some of my pocket money to buy a bottle of pop and some sweets. It was then a two mile walk to Powel's Pool in the park. Mickey had the worms to tempt Powel's Pike and I had nicked some bread from Mother's kitchen which we would crumble up and toss into the water as ground bait. Did pike like worms and fresh bread ? We hoped so.

We would talk about what had happened at school the previous week but school was always boring so it never gave way to an exciting topic of conversation.

"Did you listen to Pick of the Pops on the radio last night ?" I asked Mickey.

He had.

"So what's your favourite song ?"

"It's not in the chart now but I like Donna by Richie Valens. One day I will have a girlfriend," Mickey said, "I hope her name will be Donna."

"We go to an all-boys school," I explained, "not easy to meet up with girls."

"But you've got a sister, she must have friends you could chat up."

"My sister is three years older than me. The man is the boss, he can't be that if his girlfriend is older than he is."

"I don't have a sister," Mickey said. He then paused, smiled and completely changed the subject. "Do you think the Powel's Pool Pike is male or female ?"

"Male of course."

"If he has a girlfriend, if he has a wife then when we catch him she will become a widow."

"Oh dear, what a shame, never mind."

One day we will have girlfriends, one day. Both of us. I don't care what mine is called, why did Mickey have his hopes fixed on someone by the name of Donna ?

"Don't argue with her," Sis said. "You know she is mentally deaf. If Mother insists we all go out with Auntie Alice for the day on Saturday just go fishing with Mickey on Sunday."

I was going to have to let Mickey down but the Powel's Pool Pike would have another day to wait until we landed it.

I did not go fishing with Mickey Rig on Sunday. I never went fishing with Mickey Rig again. I never went fishing with anyone again. It was thought that Mickey had an epileptic fit, perhaps brought on by excitement. He was found floating face down in the water and when pulled out artificial respiration did not revive him, he was already dead. On the bank next to where his rod and tackle box were found there was a pike fish.

I did not go to Mickey' funeral, it was a quiet family affair and I am not sure if his father was allowed out of prison to attend. He was buried in the local cemetery. I did visit his grave.

Michael Rigg
Son of Dorothy and Peter Rigg
Brother of Paul

"Funny," I said aloud, "I never knew Mickey had a brother."

Peter's Magic Fountain Pen

AUTHOR'S NOTE:
This is a story I wrote in 1992 for my son's twelfth birthday. It was actually the first paperback work I had published. I hope you enjoy reading of Peter's adventures which include his family members:

Grandpa Morgan
Peter David Morgan
Richard James Morgan
Major William Edward Morgan
Colonel William Edward Morgan VC
Peter David Morgan
Mark Peter Morgan
Flight Captain Michael Ross Teach-Morgan

So off we go…..

Grandpa Morgan:
Sir Richard James Morgan QC Born 14th September 1900
The scene that met Peter when he came home from school that day meant only one thing. The house had an air of spring cleaning, even if it was mid-October, the hoover was bellowing its voice somewhere upstairs and there was the smell of fresh polish in the living room. The downstairs loo had blue stuff in the water, there were fresh flowers in the hall and the bowls of pot-pourri everywhere. That thing just had to be Grandpa Morgan.

"What time's he coming ?" Peter asked

"Said he'd be here by six o'clock," replied his mother somewhat out of breath after her battle with the vacuum cleaner. "Take your school things away, have a bath and smarten yourself up. I've got to try to organise something for dinner. Grandpa Morgan is hardly likely to appreciate the fish fingers and chips I had planned."

"Why is he coming ?"

"Since when has that man ever needed a reason for anything he does ? He just gets on an aircraft, jets half way around the world then expects everyone to drop everything and fall into place."

Peter picked up his school bag and headed towards his room. Why was it that Grandpa Morgan always brought on an attack of terminal panic in his mother ? She dreaded his visits so much and the trouble was that no one ever quite knew when he was going to turn up. Half of the time the family never knew where in the world he was. Just a telephone call giving a couple of hours notice, something which would send his mother's blood pressure to a point measurable on the Richter Scale, and then he would be there on the doorstep.

Strictly speaking, he was not Peter's grandfather at all, but his father's grandfather. Peter had no idea just how old Grandpa Morgan was but he had to be very old in spite of the highly active lifestyle he led. His son, Peter's real grandfather, had died in a car accident the day Peter had been born and his mother's father had died when Mum was a child so Grandpa Morgan had always been his only grandfather. But just how old was he ?

Peter knew that Dad was forty-two. If Dad's father had been twenty-five when Dad had been born and Grandpa Morgan twenty-five when his son had been born, that would make Grandpa Morgan, Peter paused in his calculating, ninety-two ! That was old, even ancient. Ninety-two, it was an incredible age.

Peter did not know it, but his estimation of Grandpa Morgan's advance age was not all that far from being right although his method of calculating the figure was a little out of line. He loved his great-grandfather so very dearly, there was a special bond between them that spanned four generations. It was not because he was rich or famous, although Peter was not beyond boasting from time to time to his friends at school about his celebrated relation, but simply because he found him the most wonderful and fascinating person in the whole world. The calculation of Grandpa Morgan's age suddenly frightened Peter, posing questions he had never before thought of. How much longer could he live ? Life without him would not be the same.

Sir Richard Morgan's tale was not one of rags to riches, far from it, he was born into a family which had at its head The Right Reverend Doctor James Edward Morgan, Bishop of Colchester. Doctor Morgan had two daughters, both much older than Grandpa and long since dead but just the one son, Peter's great-grandfather. This son was sent to school in one of the nation's most famous and expensive public schools before going on to Oxford University where he read law. Shortly after her coronation the Queen selected Grandpa Morgan as one of her Queen's Councillors, Learned in the Law, and twenty years later again he knelt before her this time to receive a knighthood. It was not the legal profession, however, that earned him his title, or for that matter his vast fortune, but his becoming one of the world's best-selling authors of all time.

It was a career taken up quite late in life and certainly not until well after the death of The Right Reverend Doctor James Edward Morgan who certainly would have frowned upon such a frivolous occupation but since he had first put pen to paper Grandpa Morgan's books had been in the top selling lists, remaining there for decades. Several had been turned into films and Peter always overfilled with silent pride when he saw the credits roll up on the TV: *Original Story by Sir Richard Morgan.* Of late he had turned to writing crime thrillers and a series featuring one of his characters, Inspector Blackwell, was currently running on ITV. Even at his advanced age Grandpa Morgan was still turning out novels at the rate of two a year..

"Peter, Peter have you finished in the bathroom yet ? Janet's home and waiting to get in there."

Finished ? Gosh he had hardly started. "What about the other bathroom ?"

"I'm about to go in there."

What chaos Grandpa's visits caused to the tranquillity of the Morgan home.

"Won't be long." But he was.

Peter passed Janet in the hallway and could not avoid her scolding. "Thank you very much little brother, so kind of you at long last ! What's the matter with you ? What's the matter with you ? Don't you want me to make myself look good for the old man then ? Or are you afraid of losing your place as his favourite great-grandchild ? He must be a hundred if he's a day and just can't go on for ever even if all his books do. You may be OK but the rest of us don't want him to cut us out of his will at this late stage do we ? Not after Mother's worked so hard all these years to secure our inheritance !"

Peter hated the way she was speaking but he had heard it before and it was not out of character. Big sisters were born to be unkind but surely she wasn't interested in Grandpa only because of all his money. No, it couldn't be true that was why his mother always made such a fuss when he visited, but was it ? Could it be possible ?

The telephone rang. It was Dad. "Peter, is Mum there ?"

"She's in the bath."

Dad was a little relieved that his wife could not come to the phone but guilty at having put his son in the role of messenger, he knew exactly what his wife's reaction would be. "Look, tell her I've been delayed at the hospital, will you. I doubt I'll be home much before eight."

Eight ! Thank you very much Dad ! Peter knew exactly what his mother would say to that piece of information.

"OK, I'll tell her."

"Thanks Son, I'm sorry."

He had hardly put the phone down when the doorbell rang. Being the sole person in the house not immersed in a bath full of water he had no alternative but to answer it. There, in all his considerable glory, stood Grandpa Morgan. Peter glanced at his watch, Grandpa was early, very early.

"Grandpa," Peter exclaimed with delight at seeing his favourite relative again and at the same time searching his brain for a way to explain the absence of his mother. "We weren't expecting you until six."

"Never too early to see my favourite great-grandson. Come to think of it my only great-grandson."

Grandpa Morgan did not wait to be invited in, he never waited to be invited to do anything, but made his own way into the living room. He was dutifully followed by a chauffeur holding a large blue suitcase in each hand.

"Just put them down, Paul, my grandson here will take them up to my room for me. You can go off now. Drive back to the London flat and I'll telephone you when I'm ready for you to come back to collect me.

"Very good, Sir Richard."

"Right then, my fine young fellow, just what have you been doing with yourself since I last saw you ?"

"Nothing much," Peter confessed, "just school."

"Just school, you poor boy, that doesn't sound very interesting. Now, I've just come back from a month in San Francisco. It's a wonderful city, you must go there some time."

"Don't they have earthquakes there ?"

"Earthquakes, theatres, opera, fine restaurants and everything else a man could possibly want," Grandpa chuckled.

"I think I'd better let Mum know that you are here," Peter rose nervously anticipating his mother's reaction and he hadn't yet told her about Dad being late home from work. "She won't be long, I think she is still in the bath."

He thought he might just possibly have heard his mother swear through the bathroom door when he told her of their visitor's early arrival. He was certain he heard she swore when he explained that Dad wouldn't be home until eight.

"Sir Richard," Mum beamed, arms outstretched. "How simply lovely to see you again. I do apologise for keeping you, we weren't expecting you quite so early. Janet will be down to join us in a little while."

"Lovely to see you too, my dear, but I hope my unexpected visit has not caused you to go to any trouble."

"Oh, no, of course not, not at all."

"Liar," Peter thought. He did not like the way his mother was falling over herself to be nice to Grandpa Morgan when less than an hour ago she was cursing his visit with every breath. Perhaps it was nerves or was it something else ? Was Janet right in what she had said ?

"I am afraid David has been held up at the hospital so I wasn't planning to eat until about eight. Will that be all right with you ?"

"Penalty of being such a fine surgeon. Whatever time you plan to eat will suit me and don't you go to any trouble. No trouble at all, please. Beans on toast would be perfectly fine for me."

Peter doubted his great-grandfather had ever eaten beans on toast in his entire life and could not picture his mother serving them on the best china in the family dining room. What a nightmare.

"Now, could Peter possibly help me upstairs with my bags and then I've got something I would like to talk to him about."

"Sure Grandpa, this way."

The old man took his time walking up the stairs and into the bedroom. He closed the door behind them and turned the key in the lock. Peter was puzzled, why had he done that ?

"Peter sit down. I need to talk to you." Grandpa Morgan was speaking quietly and was strangely serious. It made Peter feel just a little uncomfortable but he did as he was told.

"No need to look quite so worried my young grandson. What I have to say is very important but nothing at all to be afraid of."

"I'm not afraid."

"Apprehensive then, now listen. I have just made a new will, you know what a will is Peter, don't you ?"

"Yes, Grandpa."

"Well I'm going to die next year and…"

Peter began to protest, trying to say that Grandpa Morgan had a long time left to live but the old man silenced him with a gentle wave of the hand.

"Within twelve months of today, Peter, I will be dead. You mustn't be sad, I'm ninety-two already."

So Peter's calculations had been correct.

"In my will I am going to leave you these." He took from his pocket a pen and a folded sheet of paper. He placed them on the bed. Peter went to pick them up.

"Not yet, Peter, just leave them for the moment. In need to explain to you what they are and how to use them. My father explained their use to me and his father to him. My own son is dead and your father, my grandson is a highly successful man in his own right so he won't need them. I have decided, therefore, to pass by two generations and leave these most valuable possessions ton you. Do you understand that much ?"

"Yes, Grandpa," Peter replied. It wasn't exactly a lie but he did not have a clue what the old man was talking about.

Grandpa smiled. "I'm not making a very good job of this am I ? You know for a man who earns his living with words I should be able to do better. For hours on the plane coming over I tried to decide how to put things. Let me try to explain. Have you ever heard of Captain Henry Morgan ?"

"Wasn't he a pirate ?"

"Among other things, he most certainly was. He was one of the most feared pirates of all time. At his height he had thirty-seven ships and two thousand men under his command. When he retired from piracy he lived a perfectly respectable life as Governor of Jamaica and died in his bed. Tio die in your own bed was something quite rare for a pirate."

Peter listened with interest. He thought he knew perhaps what Grandpa was about to say.

"Peter Henry Morgan was your ancestor. He lived thirteen generations ago in the family. You can work out how many great-greats that is, but he was your grand-father."

That was quite exciting. "Are you going to write a book about him then Grandpa ?"

"No, Peter I am not planning to write a book about him although the idea is a good one. You can look at that sheet of paper now."

Peter picked up and unfolded the sheet, turning it round to read the writing. Written in his grandfather's mown hand it was titled: *The Morgan family Line – Male Heirs 1649+*

"You must promise me, Peter, that if I explain all of this you will not breathe a word to another living soul until the time comes for you to explain to your own son. Do you promise me that Peter ?"

"I promise."

"It is not a promise to be made lightly. It will also mean that when you get married you will have just one son, you can have as many daughters as you wish, but you will have only one son. The line must pass directly, you see there can be no complications, and you may think that is too high a price to pay."

Peter hadn't got a clue what on earth Grandpa Morgan was talking about. What was all this about sons ? He had never thought about getting married, let alone having any children of his own. He was after all only twelve years of age and had yet to find his first girlfriend, but of one thing he was sure and that was one of Grandpa's fascinating stories was about to unfold.

"Do you want me to go on Peter ?"

Peter nodded.

"Are you sure ?"

He nodded again.

"Henry Morgan," Grandpa explained, "had a son James Henry Morgan. Born on 27th January 1649. He was not so lucky as his father and was executed on Christmas Day 1700 for the crime of piracy !"

Peter settled himself into one of the bedroom chairs. Yes, this was definitely one of Grandpa Morgan's stories, perhaps it was about to be turned into a film.

"Before pirate Morgan died he gave to his son, who was Peter John Morgan, that pen."

Peter glanced from the paper he was holding to the pen and made to speak before changing his mind. He did not want to spoil Grandpa's story with such a little detail, but the old man had already anticipated him.

"I know exactly what you are thinking young Peter. That's a new pen isn't it ? So it is, but let me explain that it has not always looked like that. It's changed twice in my keeping and looked very different in old Pirate Morgan's day when he passed it to his son. That son, your ancestor who, also was called Peter Morgan, used the pen very wisely and built up a thriving shipping company. For three generations ships of the Morgan Line traded the world. Unfortunately, the next generation, James Morgan, had no interest at all in shipping. When the pen came into his keeping he sold all his shares in the Morgan Line and invested in a merchant bank. His son Edward Morgan rose to become chairman of the bank. They sound a thoroughly boring couple of people if you ask me."

Peter smiled, he knew it was required of him.

"Now Colonel William Edward Morgan, born 1820 and died at the age of seventy-one, was awarded the Victoria Cross for bravery in the Crimean War. He was my great-grandfather, the same relation as I am to you, although I never knew him. He died nine years before I was born. I have his VC medal and have left it in my will to your father, it is quite a valuable family heirloom.

"My father was Doctor Edward Morgan. Although he was never famous or rich like his father or his son, as a country doctor he put the pen to good work. I remember him from when I was a young boy and he would be so pleased to know that your father is a doctor as well, it is such a noble profession. You know, I think he did more with his life than any of the rest of us."

Peter thought that being a pirate sounded much better than being a doctor.

"My own father rose to high office in the Church to become Bishop of Colchester. He and I were never all that close. My mother died when I was just a boy and children never had all that much to do with their parents in those days. As soon as I was old enough I was sent away to boarding school. He didn't tell me about the pen until he was eighty-one years old then died the next year very reluctant to meet his maker. As great man of the Church he may have been, but he was not all that keen to report to head office !"

Grandpa laughed but Peter didn't fully understand the joke.

"When my father gave me the pen he told me, as I am now explaining to you, all about our ancestors. He told me, not without it half choking his pious throat, all about Pirate Morgan. It amuses me to think that the Right Reverend Doctor James Edward Morgan being descended from a pirate executed, of all days, on Christmas Day ! He explained to me that the pen ensured success in the chosen career of its owner. It had given him success in the Church, his father in medicine and his grandfather in the army. He told me that I was to pass it on to my son and he to his son. He explained that each son in turn would have only one son, daughters did not matter. The pen would then provide a direct line within the family, direct all the way to Pirate Morgan and the seventeenth century. He also told me that once the owner had passed on its secrets to the next generation he would be dead within a year."

"My father was dead within a year and I often wonder what kind of a time God gave him when he got to Heaven. So you see, Peter, now that I have told you the family secret I also will be dead within a year."

"No Grandpa ! No !" Peter protested.

"I am an old man, Peter, and my time is long overdue. When my father gave me the pen I was already a successful barrister with a thriving practice. He hoped it would ensure my becoming Lord Chief Justice of England but I had suffered enough of the law with its dusty old court rooms and stuffy legal books. So when it came to my keeping I retired and took up writing. My career as an author has now become much longer than my career in the law and I don't regret any of it. I would rather tell a good story any day than sit in judgement and send some poor old lag off to prison for twenty years. Besides the pay is much better."

"I had planned to give the pen to my own son, John, on his birthday but that was the very day he was killed. I did love him but the silly fool never was much of a driver. He may have been able to command fighter aircraft but in a car he was a menace. The accident was entirely his own fault and fortunately no one else was hurt, but I do miss him. You were born on the same day, fourteenth of September, that he died and I vowed there and then that the pen should be yours. Your father doesn't need it so you shall have it. Will you use Pirate Morgan's pen wisely my young Peter ?"

Peter managed a rather confused, "yes."

"No doubt when you come to pass it on it will have become some pocket, computerised word processor. It was a feather quill when Pirate Morgan stole it all those years ago. Just use it wisely, and one last thing nothing to do with the pen really but, since Pirate Morgan, this family has developed a kind of tradition in passing the Christian name of the father on to the son as a second Christian name. I am Richard, your grandfather was John Richard and your father David John. Your son must take the name of Peter as his second Christian name. Do you promise to continue the tradition ?

Peter agreed. He hoped the tale was nothing more than the plot for one of Grandpa's new books but he wasn't quite sure.

Grandpa picked up the pen and took the sheet of paper from Peter. With care he placed them both inside his jacket pocket. "The next time you see these I'll be dead and they will have been left to you in my will. No need to look so glum Peter, your entire future is now safely assured. Whatever you decide to do in life you will be the very best at it. Now, don't you think we had better go back downstairs ? Your mother will be starting to wonder what on earth has become of us."

Grandpa Morgan left the next day, it was to be the last time Peter saw him, and flew back to San Francisco. He died there three weeks later. Peter cried.

THE MORGAN FAMILY LINE:
MALE HEIRS 1649 +

Henry Morgan:
Dates uncertain. Possibly Born 1635 Died 25th August 1688 Age 53 years

Pirate and Deputy-Governor of Jamaica

John Henry Morgan:
Born 27th January 1659 Executed 25th December 1700 Age 41 years
Pirate

Peter John Morgan:
Born 17th May 1678 Died 4th July 1720 Age 41 years
Ship Owner

William Peter Morgan:
Born 4th January 1700 Died 11th June 1760 Age 60 years
Ship Owner

Frederick William Morgan:
Born 21st November 1732 Died 30th December 1755 Age 43 years
Ship Owner

James Frederick Morgan:
Born 11th June 1764 Died 11th May 1821 Age 57 years
Director of Willis and Patterson Merchant Bank

Edward James Morgan:
Born 28th February 1790 Died 16th August 1851 Age 61 years
Chairman of Willis and Patterson Merchant Bank

Colonel William Edward Morgan VC:
Born 11th November 1820 Died 21st December 1851 Age 71 years
Army Officer

Doctor Edward William Morgan:
Born 7th January 1845 Died 11th February 1910 Age 65 years

Doctor

Right Reverend Doctor James Edward Morgan:
Born 6th May 1870 Died 7th June 1952 Age 82 years
Bishop of Colchester

Sir Richard James Morgan QC:
Born 14th September 1900
Barrister at Law

Wing Commander John Richard Morgan DFC:
Born 21st April 1925 Died 14th September 1980 Age 55 years
RAF Officer

David John Morgan:
Born 3rd November 1950
Consultant Surgeon

Peter David Morgan:
Born 14th September 1980
Schoolboy

The story of the fountain pen bothered Peter at first and he could not get to sleep the night his grandfather told him of it. He dreamed of pirates, of a new book by Richard Morgan and a strange pen writing his future for him. The next day he wanted to tell someone but Grandpa Morgan had made him promise not to breathe a word. Why had he done that ? Because it was a plot for his next book and there was such a thing as copyright. Was it ? Things needed to be kept secret, of course that was it. From then on Peter did not let it trouble him very much but couldn't help secretly hoping his family was indeed descended from pirates. It couldn't do any harm to ask about that, could it ?

"Dad ?"

"Yes."

"Were our ancestors pirates ?"

"Pirates ? No, I don't think so. They were ship owners. The Morgan Line was quite famous in the eighteenth century."

"Ship owners ?"

"Yes, until the family went into banking."

Grandpa was right.

When Grandpa Morgan died he was flown home from San Francisco to be buried alongside his wife. Funny how Peter had never thought of his having a wife but, of course, he must have. He wondered with a smile what the Right Reverend Doctor Morgan said when he met up with Grandpa in Heaven. Would he give him what for, for not becoming Lord Chief Justice of England ?   Would Grandpa tell the two ancestors who had given up the shipping business for banking that they were thoroughly boring ?   Would Pirate Morgan be waiting there to meet him hin Heaven ?

Surely not, he must have gone to – well certainly not to Heaven.

Grandpa Morgan's will was read in his solicitor's office three weeks after the funeral. There was only Peter, his Mum, Dad and sister there. In spite of Grandpa's complicated finances things had been well prepared in advance and quite simply he left everything: his London flat, holiday home in San Francisco, the VC medal that had once belonged to Colonel William Morgan and all his worldly goods with one slight exception to Peter's father.

"Congratulations Doctor Morgan," the solicitor said. "Even after the death duties have been settled you will be a very rich man."

"It's Mister Morgan," he corrected. "Surgeons are called Mister and not Doctor."

"Oh, quite correct, I am sorry. Now there is one other small bequest. To my great-grandson Peter Morgan I leave my Parker Fountain Pen and my notes explaining our family history. I have previously spoken to him about these and he will be expecting them." The solicitor looked over the top of his glasses. "Is that correct Master Peter ?"

"Yes."

"Then here you are Young Sir, one Parker Fountain Pen and a sheet of your grandfather's writing. In time anything in the great writer's own hand could become of some value."

Peter took them and offered polite thanks.

"What's it like to be rich Daddy ?" Janet bubbled excitedly, quite unable to contain herself.

"I don't want to be rich, I just want to be a good surgeon."

"But you can't refuse it," his wife chided, her voice containing a slight note of fear. "Not after all those years of having to be nice to him. He never was an easy man, you know. Strange his leaving that fountain pen to Peter, perhaps he thought he would become a famous writer as well."

"Some chance of that with the reports he brings home from school each term"

Peter did not know what he wanted to be or what he would do with the pen. His grandfather may have told him the pen brought success to its owner but he had not explained how to put it to use. He put the pen away in the bedroom to think about it. But he didn't think about it, he forgot all about it.

PETER:
PETER DAVID MORGAN BORN 14TH SEPTEMBER 1980
With the Christmas holidays came the Christmas homework and like all other schoolboys, Peter fully intended to leave every last bit of it until the night before he returned to school. He was certain he couldn't do most of it any way.

Christmas Day was its usual drag of an anti-climax. Peter was far too big for Father Christmas and the day had lost much of the magic known in former years. He gave gifts, received gifts, thanked Mum and Dad and even gave sister Janet a kiss, but only on the cheek. Lunch passed off without event and when the family settled down to watch television for the afternoon Peter took himself off to his room.

The holiday homework lay on the table and he absent maimedly picked some of it up. The sheet was a simple question and answer quiz.

"In what year did Stevenson build The Rocket ?"

Peter did not have a clue. Besides what did it matter anyway ?

Question Two: "In which year was Queen Victoria made Empress of India ?"

Who cares ?

Question Three: "In which year dis Sir Arthur Conan Doyle first publish a story about Sherlock Holmes ?"

The questions were so typical of that fool who took his class for History. He had no imagination and, although it was Peter's favourite subject, it was all too often a bore. He took up a pen and wrote in the first three dates to come into his mind: 1829 – 1876 – 1887.

Question Four: "In which year was the Second Grand Alliance with the Dutch and Austrians negotiated ?" The what with the who and when ? What possible interest could that be to anyone least of all a twelve-year old boy ? Peter wrote in 1700.

What a way to spend Christmas day ! What was that date ? There was something about that year – 1700. Christmas Day 1700 ? Yes, Peter remembered and pulled out his grandfather's sheet of paper, unfolded it and checked the date. Christmas Day 1700 John Henry Morgan executed for piracy. "Bet he wasn't interested in no Grand Alliance at the time," Peter thought, "expect his mind was on other things and it wasn't roast turkey !"

For nothing more than something to do Peter answered the remaining twenty-one questions putting in the first dates to come into his head.

"When was the Battle of Culloden ?" 1746

"In which year did Wolfe capture Quebec ?" 1759

"In which year was The Boston Tea Party ?" 1773

Twenty-five questions and twenty-five totally incorrect answers but at least it was one less item of homework. Peter put it away and went back downstairs without even realising he had used Grandpa Morgan's pen to write with.

"Well done Peter Morgan, twenty-five out of twenty-five in the Christmas History Quiz. What did you do, look them all up in the Encyclopaedia Britannica ? That's the first decent piece of History work you've done all year long. Keep it up."

"But Sir.."

The New Year was not an easy time for Peter's Dad and, in consequence, the whole family found life difficult. Inheriting a lot of money was not an effortless thing to do. There was Grandpa Morgan's London flat to be sold off and the San Francisco property to be put up for auction via American lawyers. In spite of all Janet 's protests it had to be sold. She had hopes of sun filled Californian days and endless bronzed boyfriends but it was not to be. It was, however, the need to dismiss Grandpa's housekeeper and chauffeur that caused the most pain. Although generous settlements had been made for them, on the day Dad finally paid them off Peter took himself again up to his room to avoid the uncomfortable atmosphere downstairs.

Homework offered little safety. Only that one history quiz sheet had given Peter anything above his normal average grades. It seemed that no matter how hard he tried he could never manage anything better. "I guess I am just an ordinary, average kid. How could I possibly change things even using the pen ?"

Peter did not honestly believe in the pen and never realised that he had used it to achieve the full marks. If the pen worked, *if* the pen worked , it would have been very easy for Grandpa Morgan. To become a famous writer all he had to do was to pick it up and write. What about his father ? The Bishop

? Had he held it between his hands when he prayed ? What about The Morgan Line ? Had his ancestors used it instead of a compass on their ships ? And what about Pirate Morgan ? Had he used it instead of a sword ?

Peter stopped daydreaming and looked at his homework for the evening. An essay for English: "My Family". Where did teachers get these stupid ideas for homework ? A special teachers' book *One Thousand Boring Ideas For Homework* ? If they did then he bet every teacher had their own personal copy. It wouldn't be so bad if he could get interested in the work, perhaps then he could just possibly crawl above being average. Again without fully realising it was Grandpa Morgan's pen he had in his hand, Peter started writing.

My family consists of me, by big sister and my Mum and Dad. My Dad is a doctor and he operates on people. My Mum stays at home all day and I do not like my sister very much.

He wanted to write about Grandpa Morgan, how he was a famous author and that he had left a lot of money in his will but that would not have been a good idea. Grandpa's death had been extensively reported on the news and now a season of films were running as a tribute on television. Peter tried to avoid boasting too much and at school people had heard more than enough of Sir Richard Morgan. Instead he started to write about Pirate James Henry Morgan. Suddenly the pen took on a life all of its own. He felt kind of strange, as if he were in a dream. His mind was being emptied and then refilled, peculiar memories of his childhood came back to him then went away again only to be replaced with memories of a different childhood although somehow, the same childhood. He felt sleepy and slowly closed his eyes.

"Where are those charts boy ?"

Peter opened his eyes to find himself no longer seated in his bedroom with his homework spread out before him but in an oak walled room where he sat at a small desk upon which were scattered a collection of strange looking maps.

"You boy hurry up or I'll have your ears off. The charts boy, do you think the Revenge will wait for ever ?"

Revenge, what revenge ? Peter slowly realised it was to him the orders were being shouted. He was onboard a ship. It was bizarre and yet it was not at all strange. Peter should have been doing his homework but then he should have been on the ship. Had he not been sent to collect the charts ? Was the ship not racing at speed away from the enemy ?

"Yes Captain, sorry, right away." Why did he call him Captain ?

"Well hurry up lad before I have the cook roast your ears for supper !"

Peter shuddered. "Just coming…" He had been about to say "Father." Father ?

With the correct charts firmly in his hands Peter left the room, climbed the three short steps and joined a small group of men. The wind hit his face and made him smart. Above his head yards of canvas billowed in full swell. The ship was making excellent speed.

"Took your time didn't you ? Do you think that Teach and The Queen Anne's Revenge will just sit and wait for us to finish ?" Peter knew the Queen Anne's Revenge to be the heavily armoured flagship of the Teach Fleet.

Captain John Henry Morgan unrolled the map and spread it over the top of a water barrel holding it down firmly against then wind. The final clouds in Peter's mind cleared. He was no longer Peter David Morgan aged twelve, a schoolboy with homework to finish, but Peter John Morgan son of pirate captain John Henry Morgan, buccaneer and terror of the high seas.

Captain Morgan was a tall man with long dark hair that curled in the wind. He was dressed in a long red coat trimmed in gold and black which ended just above a pair of shining leather boots. He was every inch and more a pirate. Peter's own attire was not dissimilar although his coat reached only just beyond his waist. Curiously it felt as if this was his common everyday dress.

"Captain Sir," the man who approached them was the ugliest creature Peter had ever seen. He was positively hideous and had the worst case of BO imaginable. "There's land off the larboard bow, Captain Sir."

Morgan spun round clutching the charts in his fist. "Where ? Show me !"

"Two points off the larboard bow Sir."

Peter strained his eyes but could not see anything through the haze."

"Steady as she goes, Mr Mate. Prepare for new orders in five minutes. Now leave me alone with my son for a few moments."

"Right you are Sir."

Morgan placed a heavy hand on Peter's shoulder and looked him square in the eyes. Peter tried hard to meet the gaze.

"Listen Peter, listen my son, you and the rest of the crew think we've come after treasure belonging to Edward Teach don't you ?"

"Edward Teach, Captain Blackbeard yes of course."

"Don't interrupt me Peter, that mate will be back any moment. Teach hid the treasure before taking his ship to battle off the Carolina Coast. He dare not risk losing the most precious treasure of his long and bloody career so he hid it. Pity he did not take more care who knew what he was up to. Fool ! Now we are about to steal from under his nose the most valuable pirate treasure ever known in history."

"Just how much treasure is there ?"

"There's enough to make a beggar man as rich as a king, there's uncut emeralds, bezoar stones, silver, gold and much more but none is of the least importance. The crew can have it all and divide it among themselves as they wish, ours is a bigger prize. Something that will make it possible for us both to put this life behind us for ever. It's no life running from every man-of-war with the threat of the gallows ever present to haunt your sleep."

Peter knew what his father was talking about, it was the pen, Grandpa Morgan's pen. He could smell the mate approaching before ever he saw him. That foul creature was not to be trusted, better not say anything he could overhear.

"Orders Sir ?" The mate spoke. "Care to take a look through the glass Sir ?"

Morgan placed the telescope to his right eye and sighted in the direction pointed out by the mate. "Edward Teach I have you now."

Peter looked first to the chart which his father again spread out over the water barrel and then strained his eyes but could neither see the coastline nor relate their position to the map.

"Take her to within a mile of land and anchor."

The mate barked out orders which were instantly obeyed by the small crew. In time Peter faintly made out the contour of the land.

"I have you Edward Teach, I have you now . What good's your fine Queen Anne's Revenge and all your other mighty ships when they're a thousand miles way ?"

Slowly they neared the land. Although Peter could see the coast he still could not relate it to the map. But he father could and became more and more excited muttering constantly about Edward Teach and how he had outwitted his enemy to steal the greatest pirate treasure ever.

"I bet the fool does not even realise what it is that he has got."

Again Peter smelt the mate before he saw him coming. Didn't he ever take a bath ? Although he had seen the man several times his sense of smell dulled the usually more superior sense of sight. Now for the first time he stopped to study the man and noticed the rather obvious feature that he only had one leg. In place of the other was a wooden stump. Ture, it was only a partial limb descending from just below the knee, but how ever could he have failed to notice it ? But even this was not his dominating feature, that belonged to his black piercing eyes. They sat deep inside their sockets beneath heavy brows a high forehead and striped head scarf from where they bored right inside anyone upon whom their stare was focussed. Not only did the mate's body stink of a thousand sweats but every pore oozed evil, trickery and deceit. Whatever made his father sign him on as first mate ?

"I wouldn't underestimate him if I were you Captain, Edward Teach I mean. Do you want us to anchor Sir we're just about a mile off the coast now ?"

"No, turn her into the wind and follow the coast north."

New orders were issued and again instantly obeyed. There was a definite purpose now in their mission and one the crew fully appreciated. The ship turned through ninety degrees as men nimbly scaled the rigging, pulled in the sails and set new canvas. The timbers creaked and groaned under the strain. All the time Captain Morgan glanced excitedly from chart to telescope.

"There it is Peter, look see the headland ? Mr Mate alter course. Steer west and anchor half a mile off the coast."

Another revision of sails and once more the ship creaked as the timbers moved against each other, settling into a new position as the direction of travel changed.

"Look at the chart Peter, there's the headland. See it ? We'll drop anchor in deep water and take the longboat into the beach. Once we have all the treasure the crew can take it to the ship. All we need is for them to give us a fast passage back to Jamaica and then piracy is over for ever for us. Just one thing out of Teach's treasure boy, that's all we need."

"You mean the pen ?" It was an innocent but careless remark.

Morgan was for a moment taken back. "Pen ? What pen ? What are you talking about boy ?" There was a note of fear in his voice that hinted of anger.

"Sorry, I thought you were after Teach's gold quill."

"Who told you that ? I never told you about no quill !" Morgan snapped angrily clutching at his son's shoulders. "Tell me who told you about it, tell me do you hear !"

For the first time since he found himself onboard Captain Morgan's ship Peter was frightened. Until then it had all been somehow natural that he should be there and he felt warmth towards the pirate, the warmth of a son towards his father. But now his feelings were starting to change.

"Tell me boy ! Does Teach have a spy in my crew ? Who is it ? Who is it that has betrayed us ?"

Peter tried to think. How could he tell his father about Grandpa Morgan and the history of the pen ?

"Please, Father, you're frightening me. I just knew about it that's all. A kind on instinct. No one told me, I promise. I just felt it." It was a weak attempt at an explanation but the pirate relaxed a little. "It was instinct, that's all. Honestly, Father."

"No it wasn't," an air of calm started to return to Morgan's voice, "it was destiny, destiny boy. Your feelings have confirmed all that I hoped for." He pulled Peter close to him in a paternal embrace.

Peter wanted to say something else to support his rather pathetic story, perhaps to attempt an explanation about Grandpa Morgan, when the smell of the mate descended upon them again.

"Longboat and crew are ready Sir." Peter's dislike of the man increased. He felt the mate should not be trusted and he could not abide the way he said *Sir* all the time. In was not spoken out of piratical respect for the rank of captain but... Peter paused in his writing as he thought for the right words to use.

Straight away he was back home again, writing that dreadful essay on his family. He looked about him to confirm that he was indeed in his bedroom. Yes, there was the computer, there was a poster of the Lancaster Bomber he bought on the school trip to the RAF museum and there was his homework. He was staggered at how much he had written. He read through the story. Captain Morgan, Blackbeard's treasure, the mate with the BO, they had all been very real. So, that was how his family came to have the pen, the pen he was holding in his hand. The pen he had been writing with. He started to write again.

Instantly, he was transported back. The familiar bedroom left him as his mind emptied and refilled to be replaced by a longboat closing on a golden sandy beach edged with palm trees against a blue sea. There were six of them in the boat; four crew members, Peter and his father. The mate was conspicuous by his absence, perhaps he had been left in charge of the ship and its remaining crew. Peter doubted if the entire complement consisted of more than twenty men so there was nearly one third of them there in the longboat.

The small boat pitched and tossed its way through the roaring surf until it came to a halt with a thump on the beach. Morgan was out ahead of the rest, striding up the sand with vigour and purpose. It was as if, for a short time at least, he was oblivious to the presence of everyone else. Peter chased after him. Even if they could have seen round the headland they were all much too busy to see the ship making its way along the coast towards them. It was, however, only too clear to the mate and those left onboard. Had there been any doubt, through the telescope, they would have been able to see clearly that it was the Queen Anne's Revenge.

As Morgan raced up the beach he was under the impression that Edward Teach, the evil and feared Captain Blackbeard, was a thousand miles away heading for his hunting grounds off the Carolina coast. The last place he expected him to be was on the other side of the headland making good speed towards his own ship anchored half a mile off shore.

"Teach blazed a tree to mark the spot," Morgan explained. "Everyone look out for a charred tree."

It was Peter who found it. "Here father, look." But as he ran closer he saw the skull at the foot of the trunk. He caught his breath and stopped.

"Good boy Peter ! Never mind him, If Blackbeard took the poor fellow's life then it's a certainty his ghost will be on our side against his former master. Here men, dig. It can't be very deep. Dig, dig for the riches of our good friend and kind benefactor Captain Blackbeard."

With great purpose they all dug. The chest was deeper than Morgan had imagined. He had thought the root system of the tree would have made it impossible for Teach's men to have buried it more than a few inches below the surface. The treasure was, in fact, six heat-sweated feet down. To begin with, Morgan thought he must have the wrong spot, but the freshly turned earth and the clear signs of where the tree's roots had been sawn away reassured him that his information as to the hiding place had been correct. It must have taken hours to dig the original hole and it took nearly two to uncover the chest.

Dripping sweat, they hauled it out of its hiding place. The treasure was in just a seaman's small wooden chest. The lock was not even fastened. Morgan opened the lid and all gazed upon the contents in amazed disbelief. The four crew members plunged their hands deep into the riches letting them dribble through their fingers as they dreamed of the prosperous future that was now theirs. Morgan picked up just one item and studied it with some care.

Peter smelled the mate and looked up from his crouching position by the chest to see two legs, one made of wood, approaching. But he should have been on the ship out in the bay, what was he doing there ? Before he could stand up there was a shot and one of the pirates fell dead. Peter was the only one who noticed his father slide a single item into a pocket deep inside his red coat.

Together with the mate stood ten men, all armed with muskets pointing directly at Morgan and his crew.

"Edward Teach !" Morgan exclaimed.

"You have the advantage of me Sir."

"That I do not Teach, you know exactly who I am, why else would I be here ? I can see that my loyal ship's mate has more than introduced me to you. May I presume he has shared my every word with you ?"

Teach laughed. "He is one of my closest friends."

"Perhaps you enjoy his evil stench, no doubt a fitting companion for you."

The mate made move to fire his musket but obeyed Teach's signal to wait. "Now there's no cause to be so personal and they are very brave words from a dead man. A dead man, that is, who has just dug his own grave. It would be a pity not to put something into the hole seeing how much effort you must have all put into digging it."

Another signal from Teach and the muskets were all sighted upon Morgan.

"Say your prayers."

"At least I have a God to whom I can say them, Blackbeard, which is more than you can do. When the Devil comes to take you Teach no prayer will save your soul from the damnation of Hell."

"Well if you are quite sure of your own salvation you and your men will be able to speak your pieties direct to the Almighty in person in just a few minutes time, I hope he appreciates them."

"Not the boy Teach !"

Teach paused. "No not the boy. Never let it be said that Captain Edward Teach was anything less than kind hearted towards children. He can go but run child before I change my mind."

Morgan embraced his son pushing something into his hand. "Run my son. Run and do not stop. Remember your destiny."

"Very good advice boy. Now take it."

Peter wanted to run, the future of the Morgan family for the next twelve generations at least depended upon it, but if Grandpa Morgan had been right then Pirate Morgan was not finished yet. Did he not die on a hangman's rope and not at the hands of his enemy Captain Blackbeard ? Peter was only twelve years old and Grandpa Morgan's family tree showed he would be twenty-two when his father died. Should he run ? Should he be a coward and desert his own father ? What was it Grandpa Morgan had said about living for only a maximum of a year after the secret of the pen had been passed on ? Had the pen not just been passed on to him ?

As his mind raced to calculate all the possibilities Peter stopped writing. But he heard the shots before he found himself back home in his own bedroom sweating with fear. Was Pirate Morgan dead ? Has he cheated Blackbeard out of the treasure ? He had no intention of going back to find out. Had it all been a dream or had there been some reality ?

Peter stuffed the papers of his homework together and counted up the pages. Fourteen sides, that was more than enough for any English essay. With a sense of relief and without reading a single word he had written, he put the work away. Then with extra special care he hid Grandpa's fountain pen.

RICHARD JAMES MORGAN:
BORN 14TH SEPTEMBER 1900 DIED 17TH NOVEMBER 1992

"Peter Morgan. That was a good piece of homework but not quite what I asked you to write."

"No Sir."

"You were supposed to write about your family and not some fictitious pirate adventure."

"Sorry Sir." Peter really did not want to discuss the essay.

"No need to be sorry Peter, the work in itself is almost worthy of an A grade but if in an examination you do not stick strictly to the title you will fail no matter how good it was."

"Yes Sir."

"I think, therefore, we'll settle for a B grade shall we ?"

"Thank you Sir." Even a B grade was infinitely better than his usual average E. Peter was pleased but wished he had never written the essay. He didn't really want to think any more about it.

Peter's form teacher was a kindly old lady, one who was coming towards the end of her teaching career. Peter's idea of a perfect granny. Over the lunch hour she heard all about the famous essay. After calling the afternoon register she asked him to remain behind for a few minutes.

It was common practice. If ever she wanted to scold, or more often to praise, she would ask the student to stay behind. She was one of the best teachers in the whole school and knew every one of her tutor group well. She knew that Peter had taken his Grandfather's death hard and that he was under a lot of pressure from his mother about his school work. Mrs Morgan wanted her son to leave and go to an expensive boarding school but he would never have been happy there. It was hard for him to follow in the footsteps of his successful father and famous grandfather, he needed lots of encouragement and support.

"Mr Jackson was very pleased with your story Peter. Well done."

"Thank you Mrs Green."

"I'm pleased with you Peter, keep it up and you can expect a much better report at the end of term than you received last term. Now I've got something in want to ask you. We've a new boy starting in two days time and he's joining our class. I'd like you to look after him, make him feel welcome. He's had a hard time lately, his father died last summer and his mother has decided to move house to start a new life. Things are going to be difficult for him, so he will need friends."

Poor kid, but Peter liked the idea of having to look after him. A new friend could be good, but there was to be a catch.

"His name is Christopher Teach," explained Mrs Green. "At least I think it is, the writing on this sheet of paper's not all that easy to decipher, even with my reading glasses on."

TEACH ! Peter's blood ran cold. It couldn't be. No ! His mind exploded as he thought of such a terrible possibility. Could Blackbeard possibly have chased him down through nearly three centuries ? No, of course not, that was silly, but that name – Teach. Was he after the pen ?

"Peter, are you alright ? You look ill all of a sudden. Are you poorly ? Do you want to go to Matron ?"

"No, honestly Mrs Green, I'm fine."

Teach. Christopher Teach. That name echoed about in his brain. Was this new boy descended from Captain Blackbeard, Edward Teach, just as he was descended from Pirate Morgan ? No, it was beyond all the bounds of possibility but it had to be, it was too much of a coincidence. What could, indeed what should he do ? All afternoon he could think of nothing else. By the end of school Peter had decided that the only person who could possibly offer any advice to him was Grandpa Morgan and he knew exactly what he had to do to get that help.

He tried to be patient. All through tea he waited while he sat through the family conversation. He lied about having a good day at school. Although he was proud of the grade achieved with the essay, he said nothing at all about it. Once the meal was over and the table cleared he took himself upstairs, picked up the fountain pen and started to write.

"My great-grandfather was Sir Richard James Morgan QC. He was born on 14th September 1900 and died only last year. During his lifetime he became very rich and famous…"

The sensation came more quickly this time. Peter felt his mind being emptied, memories flashing by and new thoughts filling their place. As the mist cleared he assumingly found himself in a different time.

"Peter, come and look."

"What is it Richard ?"

Once more the pen had placed him onboard a ship but this was no wooden sailing ship, it was an ocean liner. He was playing a game of makeshift cricket with another boy of similar age on the open deck. Instinctively, he knew that the other boy was Grandpa Morgan. Things had gone slightly wrong. He could not ask the help of a young boy. Grandpa Morgan had not been given the pen by his father, the bishop, until he was an old man. He would have to back and try again. Peter tried to stop writing and give up be he could not, the pen refused to let him.

"Look over there Peter, see the ice."

Peter peered out to sea but could see nothing. The cold made his eyes water. "You have better eyes than I have or else a much better imagination !"

Turning back to prepare his run up to bowl, Peter saw one of the ship's lifeboats fixed to the railings. Things had gone slightly wrong, they had gone horribly, terrifyingly and desperately wrong. This ship was the RMS Titanic !

In desperation Peter tried to stop writing but the open just would not let him. It danced over the paper in a life all of its own. He was on his way to New York with his aunt and cousin Richard Morgan, on his way to New York on board the famous Titanic. Date ? Yes what was the date ? He had learned about the loss of the Titanic in History at school. The date was Saturday 14th April 1912.

Grandpa Morgan had been on the Titanic ! He had never said anything about it. If only Peter could stop writing and return to the safety of his own bedroom in his own time. But the pen had other ideas and continued its frantic writing.

"Peter, are you going to bowl or not ?"

"What's that ice ?"

Richard patiently put down the bat and walked to stand behind his cousin. "Over there, look. Pack ice floating out to sea."

Peter could just see the ice in the dim light of the fading afternoon. It was there alright. "Richard he said," taking care not to address his cousin as Grandpa, "this ship is in great danger. It is going to sink."

"Don't be crazy Peter, the Titanic sink ? Why everyone knows she is unsinkable, she's the biggest and safest liner ever built."

"I tell you Richard this ship is going to hit an iceberg, sink and hundreds of lives will be lost."

Richard regarded his cousin's remarks at first as a poor joke and then, realising how serious he was in the way he spoke, decided it was a display of fear. "I'll fetch Mother, wait here." He dashed off to her cabin before Peter could offer any protest, returning in only a very short time with a lady who Peter knew had to be his great-great-grandmother, the wife of The Right Reverend Doctor James Edward Morgan.

"Now what's this all about Peter ?"

What a fearful lady she was. She would never believe his story. "Nothing Aunt, sorry. I was just frightened, that's all. I'm alright now."

"I should hope so too. Now I have some very exciting news for you two boys. Tonight at dinner we have been invited to dine at the first officer's table. Isn't that exciting ?" She handed a gold trimmed invitation card to the boys. Peter read it trembling with fear.

FIRST OFFICER WINSTON TEACH REQUESTS THE
PLEASURE OF
MRS JAMES MORGAN AND HER COMPANIONS TO DINE
AT HIS TABLE TONIGHT 8PM IN THE FIRST CLASS
DINING ROOM
PLEASE PRESENT THIS CARD TO THE STEWARD UPON
ARRIVAL

Teach, that name again ! First Officer Teach, second in command of the Titanic ? Blackbeard was indeed chasing the Morgan family through the centuries. Peter knew he had to do something. He must save Grandpa Morgan from the most famous maritime disaster of all time.

Peter and Richard were sharing a first class cabin while Aunt Morgan had a stateroom all to herself. She had brought her maid along in order that her every domestic need could be catered for. The maid was accommodated only in a third class cabin and had to share that with the maid of a rich American lady. The furnishings in the first class cabins were elaborate and expensive, obviously being the Bishop of Colchester was a very highly paid occupation.

"I can't wait until I get back to school," Richard explained. "What a time I'm going to have telling all my friends that I dined at the first officer's table on the mighty Titanic."

"That won't be all you'll have to tell them," Peter whispered softly.

"Not as good, of course, as the captain's table but you have to be a millionaire or royalty to be invited to join Captain Smith."

"If you only knew," thought Peter. "If you only knew.!"

"Richard, I want you to promise me something."

"Yes."

"Stay very close to me tonight please. I don't want you ever to be far away."

"You're not still frightened that this ship is going to sink are you Peter ?"

"Richard, you are my best friend as well as my cousin so please do as I ask. I know this ship is going to sink. Don't ask me how but I know so please trust me."

Richard was starting to become worried about his cousin. Of course the Titanic could never sink but why was Peter acting so strangely ? It wasn't like him. Could it be a form of seasickness. Perhaps he should see the ship's doctor.

As Peter considered the vast size of the Titanic he did wonder if it was all a mistake, but no it couldn't be. The Titanic struck an iceberg on her maiden voyage and sank. It was in all the history books and everyone knew about it. This was her maiden voyage, her only voyage, there could be no mistake !

Dinner was at eight o'clock and Aunt Morgan, Richard and Peter were on time. Proudly they presented their invitation to the steward who escorted them to First Officer Teach's table. It was close to the captain's table where the boys could see the great man with his guests. First Officer Teach looked every bit as splendid in his dress uniform although he was much younger than the captain. He took Aunt Morgan by the hand and showed her to her seat. He patted Richard and

Peter each on the head. Richard glowed with pride but Peter went cold and felt shivers run down his spine.

He studied Teach's face and tried to see if there was any resemblance with the evil Captain Blackbeard but he could not tell. Blackbeard was, of course, as his name suggest a bearded man while this first officer was clean shaven.

"Delighted you could join us," Teach said to Aunt Morgan.

"So kind of you to invite us and such an honour for the boys. I am sure they cannot wait to tell all of their school friends when they get home."

"That you Sir," Richard added politely. "May I ask you some questions about the ship ?"

"What would you like to know young man ?"

"How many lifeboats does the Titanic have ?" Peter interrupted.

"Lifeboats !" Teach laughed loudly startling Peter. "Now why ever would the Titanic need lifeboats ? Do you think we are going to sink ?"

Aunt Morgan glared at Peter, it was a stare of a thousand reprimands. She said nothing, but her eyes did all and more of the scolding needed. "My nephew has never boon onboard a liner before," she apologised, "he is a little frightened I fear."

"Let me assure you my young dinner guest," Teach turned to smile at Peter. "If anything happens to this ship I will personally oversee your safety."

The assembled guests laughed with Teach and nothing more was said. Teach made polite conversation with the adults, talking about the ship's speed, direction and estimated docking time in New York.

"And what takes you to New York, Mrs Morgan ?"

Aunt Morgan smiled. "My mother was an American from Boston. She moved to England to marry my father. I am going in search of my ancestors. My Husband could not get away to travel with me so he suggested I take the boys for company. I am told that Boston is very beautiful in the spring."

"That it is, Mrs Morgan. I am quite certain you will find it totally delightful."

The food was splendid although Peter did not recognise several of the dishes. They were unlike anything served up at school. All of the food on board had been good, but that at Teach's table was extra special. When the waiter offered the boys wine Aunt Morgan, surprisingly, agreed to their having just one glass. For a while Peter's attention was diverted from the fate that was waiting for them, but he could never put out of his mind the fact that their host for the evening was named Teach. Several times during the meal the handsome first officer looked over to the boys and winked. Richard stored it up in his mind to add to the story when he returned home, but Peter could only cringe every time Teach looked his way. It was as if teach knew who Peter was and exactly why he was onboard the Titanic.

Peter saw the steward approach Captain Smith's table. He watched the captain excuse himself and then took a look at the grand clock on the dining room wall. It was six minutes past nine. The steward then walked over to First Officer Teach and spoke quietly to him.

"My guests," Teach rose, "I must ask you to excuse me for just a short while. The Captain wishes to see me on the bridge. Nothing to worry about I can assure you but the radio room has received a number of iceberg warnings, If they are still about in the morning you should be able to see them."

"Will this slow the ship's speed Mr Teach ?"

"I doubt it very much Madam. Fear not, we will make New York in excellent time, this is a very fast ship. On our next crossing we intend making an all-out attempt on the speed record and then to see that no one ever beats us."

"Slow the ship down," Peter thought. "Within a few hours one of the icebergs would stop the Titanic dead in her tracks, rip her heart out and send her to the very bottom of the ocean."

Peter tried to stop writing. He needed time to work out a plan to save Grandpa Morgan but the pen refused every attempt to give up.

Teach was not away from the table for very long. When he returned he explained that there was a large icefield ahead of them with some pretty spectacular bergs. Extra lookouts had been posted so there was no need to slow down. They were still on schedule to dock in New York on time. He explained that there would certainly be icebergs about the next morning when it was daylight and suggested passengers use their cameras to capture them to show to friends and families at home. Peter listened to all he said and started to form his plan to save Grandpa Morgan.

Dinner did not finish until well after ten o'clock when both boys felt they had eaten like regular trenchermen. Peter had studied the Titanic in history at school, it was one of the few subjects that interested him, so he knew he had the date correct. The liner hit the iceberg shortly before midnight on Saturday 14th April. Only twenty-five minutes later the order was given to swing out the lifeboats. It was this short space of time that would make peter's plan possible. Before getting into bed he put ready everything he needed and hoped that Richard did not drop off to sleep too quickly.

" Richard, are you asleep ?"

"Not yet."

"Are you tired ?"

"No, I'm still excited about meeting the first officer. Besides I think I have eaten too much, my belly aches."

"I'm sorry about being so silly earlier, about the ship sinking I mean."

"Don't worry about it. I think I'm going to be sick."

"No you don't, think of something else. I'm quite looking forward to seeing those icebergs in the morning aren't you ?"

"I wonder if there are any out there now." Grandpa was playing into his hands, or was it destiny exerting its influence ? I could do with a walk. I wish I hadn't eaten those three helpings of pudding."

"Let's sneak out and take a look," Peter crossed his fingers tightly.

"Mother will kill us if she finds out. She says the night air is not good for you but I'd rather be sick on deck than in here."

"She'll never know, her maid left ages ago, she'll be fast asleep by now." For all he knew Aunt Morgan's maid was still with her in the cabin next door but it was a risk he had to take.

Peter slid out of bed and started to dress. "Come on then, it'll be a laugh if nothing else, like the midnight feats in the dorm at school."

"Don't talk about food please."

Peter offered a silent prayer of thanks and hastily dressed before Richard could change his mind. The boys closed the cabin door behind them as quietly as possible, crept to the end of the passage and out of the reach of Aunt Morgan. Once at a safe distance they ran outside on to the deck.

"Let's try the boat deck, should be able to get a good view from there," Peter suggested.

The boat deck was just about the worst possible place to try to look for icebergs. The superstructure of the davits holding the lifeboats made it almost impossible to see anything. It was a moonless night but full of stars. Strange.

"This is no good," Richard protested. "Let's try the promenade deck."

"No, wait, Richard look."

Richard turned to follow Peter's direction but saw nothing before the blow hit the back of his neck. Peter had put his two fists together and struck his dear friend the hardest blow he could manage. "Sorry Grandpa," he apologised, hoping his beloved relative was not too badly hurt. But he was only stunned and Peter had to move quickly. He tied his grandpa's ankles together and then bound his hands. For good measure he looped the rope between the tied hands and feet, pulling them behind his back. Richard started to groan as he came to. Before he could be heard Peter gagged him. He hoped that Richard would not be sick and choke.

Richard looked through a daze of amazement at his cousin, failing to understand why his best friend had just attacked him and tied him up. He tried to speak but the gag was too tight. He struggled but could not move. Peter refused to let their eyes meet but whispered, "I'm sorry but this is the only way I could think to save you."

Richard's eyes opened wide and although he could not meet his cousin's gaze, looked deep into his face. He could see the love Peter so obviously had for him.

"Trust me Richard, trust me."

Richard nodded.

"I am going to lift you up into one of those lifeboats. You will understand why one day but I can't tell you now. What I can tell you is that within a few hours this ship will sink. It will…"

Neither of the boys saw the iceberg, neither of then realised the mighty Titanic was desperately trying to change her course, neither boy felt the impact of the collision but both heard it. A thundering rumble that was accompanied by a shower of ice. Huge blocks crashed to the deck like giant hailstones. Richard struggled in an attempt to free himself. There was no longer any need to keep his friend bound up so Peter began to untie the knots. But he had fastened them so well it was difficult to undo many of the ropes.

The dull throbbing of the ship's engines that had constantly been in the background ever since they had left Southampton suddenly ceased. While they remained the only two on the boat deck, below they could hear shouts of excitement, excitement without any sense of fear. It sounded as if a party was going on along the promenade deck.

As Peter finally released Richard's hands and untied the gag Richard spluttered. "I believe you Peter, I don't know how or why you knew, but I believe you now."

The two boys climbed the superstructure into one of the lifeboats and secured the canvas over them. At 12.25am Captain Smith, knowing only too well that his ship was dying, ordered the lifeboats to be run out. At 12.45am the first of them was lowered. The boys were in the third boat to get away. Nobody questioned their presence in the boat when the cover was taken off and loading began, there was too much confusion to bother about two small boys. Peter thought he saw First Officer Teach standing in the boat deck as they were lowered away. He could not be certain, it was too dark, but he thought he saw him wave.

Richard said nothing as they moved away from the stricken liner. It was all like a dream, a very bad dream. Peter also said nothing, for it too was a dream but at least Grandpa Morgan was safe. Safe to grow up and to grow old, safe to become the grandpa he had known and loved so very much.

At 218am the Titanic sank beneath the ocean taking hundreds of souls to their watery graves. Among them First Officer Winston Teach. At 2am Peter stopped writing and returned home to the safety of his own bedroom and his own time.

MAJOR WILLIAM EDWARD MORGAN:
BORN 11TH NOVEMBER 1920 DIED 21ST DECEMBER 1891
Grandpa Morgan may have been safe but Peter was now more convinced than ever that Edward Teach was perusing

his family down the ages. Soon he would have to meet up with Christopher Teach. What would he do ? His attempt to contact Grandpa Morgan for help had failed, but were there any other of his ancestors who could offer assistance ? He had to get help from somewhere.

Peter took again his grandfather's handwritten family tree. Henry John Morgan, Frederick Morgan ? It would be wise to avoid pirates. Three generations who ran the Morgan Shipping Line. A possibility but perhaps not the best chance of any help. James Morgan, Edward Morgan ? They were the stuffy bankers Grandpa Had called boring. But what about William Morgan ? He had won the Victoria Cross and risen to become colonel of his regiment, he sounded like Peter's best chance.

Peter studied the family tree again. Edward Morgan died in August 1851, so his son William Morgan must have known about the pen at the time. Peter needed to be careful that he was not transported back to find his great-great-great-great grandfather as a twelve year old boy the way he had found Grandpa Morgan. He thought for a moment. He also wanted to be sure he found his ancestor at a time when he was more than familiar with the pen and its special powers. Better add on a few years just to be certain. When was it William Morgan had won the VC ? Peter's new plan started to form in his mind. Picking up the pen he wrote.

"My great-great-great-great grandfather," he took care to get the correct number of greats, "was an army officer who served in the Crimean War where he won the Victoria Cross. At the time…"

Peter shut his eyes as the changes were made. When he opened them again he knew exactly who he was. The transformation was taking less time than when he had first used the pen and his mind was becoming clearer much more quickly with each change. He was now another Peter, still aged twelve, but a drummer-messenger boy in the 4th Light Dragoons. He stood on a small rise looking down on the regiment's camp neatly pitched upon the plains above Balaclava.

Rows of round white tents stood to attention each with its side walls rolled up to reveal kit immaculately stacked as if waiting inspection. Wooden huts served as mess halls while fenced areas accommodated hundreds, if not thousands, of cavalry horses. It looked too peaceful and tranquil. Peter found himself with an uneasy feeling of fear. It was a fear he had known before but could not be exactly certain where or when, something about being on a ship that sank. No, that possibly could not be, the ship that had brought him safely to the Crimea had docked in Cossack Bay three months ago. Perhaps it was a fear of being found out. Peter had lied about his age, everyone thought he was much older. Yes, that would be it. He tried to put it out of his mind, they were hardly going to send him home now and falsifying you age was not a court martial offence.

But it was no use standing about thinking, Peter had to find William Morgan. He knew he was not yet Colonel but Major Morgan but Major Morgan commanding the Third Division. He set out to look for his ancestor.

Major William Morgan lay back against a kit bag. At his side was an array of empty mess tins. Morgan was holding out his right arm presenting an enamel mug to his batman.

"Fill it up John. This may not be cut crystal but that's still a mighty fine vintage."

"Yes Sir."

Peter waited quietly standing to attention. Major Morgan was every inch of him a haughty gentleman, the mis-product of an upper class breeding system. He wore his hair parted and waved and had a semi-beard about his chin. His eyebrows bushed above a pair of cunning eyes. He raised the wine and sniffed the bouquet, savouring it before sipping gently. The batman waited patiently for his master's approval.

"Very good John."

"Thank you Sir."

"How clever of you to find such a wonderful wine out here in the middle of nowhere, What's that boy staring at ? Who is he ? What does he want ? Ask him John."

"What do you want boy ?"

"Could I speak with Major Morgan please ?"

"With me ! What could a drummer boy possibly want with me ? Are you bearing a message lad ? If you are then present it in the approved way as set out in battalion orders or I'll report you to your commanding sergeant."

"No Sir, I haven't brought a message Sir. It's something of a personal nature, Major."

"A personal matter, eh ? Private Teach, send this boy on his way, box his ears if you like but stop him bothering me."

Teach again ! That name ! Another failed attempt.

Not only was Major Morgan quite the most objectional person Peter had ever met but to top it all his batman was called Teach. There seemed very little point in trying to speak any more with him, he'd never listen and besides Edward Teach had got there before him.

"Come along lad back to your own quarters. Don't trouble the Major, after all he's a very busy man you know." Teach spoke kindly, putting a hand on Peter's shoulder to lead him away. Unlike the time when Winston Teach had patted him on the head he did not feel uncomfortable but strangely secure.

"You shouldn't mind the Major, it's just his way. Now is there anything I could do for you ? You look very young and homesick."

Peter did not answer.

"Look lad, if you need a friend you can always turn to me, I've got a boy of my own at home."

"Thank you Sir."

"You don't have to call me Sir, my name's John. What's your name ?"

"Peter."

"How old are you Peter ?"

"Twelve."

"Twelve years old ! Gee, you shouldn't even be here. Is that what you wanted to see the Major about ? Did you lie about your age when you signed on ?"

"Yes, I did lie but I don't want to go home. Please don't tell anyone about my age, they think I am fifteen years old and I don't want them to send me home."

"You can trust me Peter, besides they'll not send you home now." Somehow Peter knew that he could trust him. He had warmed to Major Morgan's batman but that name – Teach.

Peter reported back on duty and was immediately despatched as a runner with a letter from the commanding officer. "Deliver that to Major Morgan."

"Yes Sir."

Any other officer, any other assignment, why did it have to be Major Morgan ? Fate was unkind but Peter could not avoid the duty.

"Major Morgan," Peter snapped to attention and saluted.

"You again ? I thought my batman sent you away."

"A letter for you Sir." Peter offered the letter but Major Morgan made no move to take it.

"Put it down little boy, put it down and go away."

"But it's urgent Sir."

"Don't tell me what's urgent boy. I'll decide what's urgent and what's not. Now go away before I have you whipped."

Peter did as he was ordered. That Major Morgan was a mean one. Perhaps he should stop writing and give up any hope of being able to talk to him. Perhaps he should try someone else, but who ? Although he considered the possibilities Peter did not stop. It was not the pen this time that continued but Peter himself. He was curious and wanted to know a little more both about Major Morgan and his batman Private John Teach.

Peter had eight more messages to run before his duties for the day ended. None of them, thank goodness, took him anywhere near Major Morgan's part of the camp. His own accommodation was comprised of one of the white bell-tents which he shared with nine other boys. Ten kit-bags and ten wooden camp beds left very little room for anything else. Peter lay back on his bed and thought.

If he stopped writing he would have to face Christopher Teach at school without any idea of how to confront him. Major Morgan was not likely to offer him any advice and despite his kindness he could hardly ask his batman. What a pompous snob his great-great-great-great-grandfather was.

How did he manage to win the VC ? He drifted through these and many other questions until he eventually fell asleep.

All night Peter slept deeply. He dreamed he was a twelve year old boy living more than a hundred years into the future. His father was a doctor and they lived in a comfortable house but strangely with no servants. The house was full of familiar and yet quite unfamiliar machines. Peter thought he should know what a television set was but what was a camcorder, a microwave and a motor car ? He was not at all certain, it was all very confusing. Although he had never been to school in his life he dreamed of being in a class with a teacher called Mrs Green and a boy, Christopher Teach, who was his arch enemy. Teach – wasn't that the name of Major Morgan's batman ? Perhaps Christopher was his son, didn't he say he had a boy at home ?

The sound of a trumpet disturbed his sleep. Peter turned over. He thought he could hear voices of other boys and then a much older and a much louder voice boomed through the canvas.

"Out of bed, you young scum. Ablutions, breakfast and then report for duty."

Ten boys simultaneously groaned and crawled out of their beds. Peter shivered as he washed in ice cold water with soap that felt as if it was made of sand. Breakfast was hot and filling but totally without any taste. Peter had a faint recollection that he hated porridge but he ate all he was given.

His first duty of the day again involved the dreaded Major Morgan. Peter found him at his breakfast, a very different meal to that he and his fellow messenger boys had just eaten.

"You again ! Wretch, what is it this time ?"

Peter saluted smartly. "Colonel's compliments, Sir, and would you please join him in his tent at eight o'clock."

"You would think would you not that the modern British Army could find a better way of transporting its messages about the camp than by using a worm like you."

Peter did not answer, it was not required of him.

"A worm, a lower life form, that's what you are. Be off back to the gutter whence you came and stop standing there littering the space before my eyes. Private Teach ! Where is my batman ? Private Teach !"

Major William Morgan was going to be of no help at all, Peter was sure of that. He stopped writing. The pen offered no resistance and he was safely home again.

Breakfast in the Morgan Home was very different to that served by the field kitchen on the plains of Balaclava. For once the whole family was together at the table.

"Dad ?"

"Yes Peter," his father looked up from a plate of bacon and egg to answer his son.

"You remember that Victoria Cross Grandpa Morgan left you."

Peter's Dad nodded. "It's in a safety deposit box at the bank but funny you should mention it, I've just been reading about it."

"Can you tell me about it then ?"

"What do you want to know ?"

"Everything." Peter paused then added, "If it is in the bank does that mean it is valuable ?"

"Every VC is valuable Peter but this one is of special significance as it was only the third ever awarded and was cast out of metal cut from a Crimean War cannon."

"How did our ancestor win it ?"

"Now that's quite a story, he saved the life of his batman."

William Morgan had saved the life of Private Teach ?

"How ?"

"Full of questions this morning aren't you, just as well I know the answers. During the Crimean War there was a terrible cavalry charge. William Morgan shouldn't even have been there but somehow he and his batman were with the Light Brigade when a foul up of order sent them charging into the enemy. Four hundred men, two thirds of the force, were cut down. William, risking his own life, infact he lost an arm as a result, took his batman back to camp and safety. With his own arm useless, cut and bleeding he took the batman to the camp hospital where none other than Florence Nightingale nursed them both back to health."

"So the batman survived ?"

"Oh yes. He stayed with old Morgan right through his army career. When he retired the batman became his personal valet. He died just one week after his master."

Peter was fascinated but it didn't sound much like the Major Morgan he knew.

"Like I said when the Victoria Cross was introduced for bravery in times of war, William Morgan was one of the first to be honoured. Each winner was also awarded a lifetime pension of one hundred pounds a year. William Morgan when he received the money each year gave it to his batman. It was said that in later life the two, although master and servant, became very close friends. You know, Peter, old William Morgan must have been a rather special man.

Peter doubted that. His encounter with Major Morgan showed him to be a pompous bully. Surely Morgan and Teach could never have become friends. Not only were they so different but it would not fit the theory about Blackbeard chasing the pen down the ages. Yet, Peter remembered how he had warmed to Teach, perhaps things had changed.

During the lunch break at school Peter went into the library and, with the help of the school librarian, looked up the Victoria Cross in the Encyclopaedia Britannica.

VICTORIA CROSS. A bronze cross inscribed *FOR VALOUR* with a crimson ribbon, was instituted on 29th January 1865 as a reward for conspicuous bravery in war.

There was also a small picture showing a light brown cross with a lion standing upon a crown. Underneath were written the words *For Valour.*

Peter closed the book. "How could I find out about one of the winners ? He won it for saving his batman's life during a cavalry charge in the Crimean War ?"

"That would have been at The Battle of Balaclava." The librarian directed Peter to another book: Steinbeck's Dictionary of British History.

Badonicus…Bagdad…Bail… Balaclava – The Battle of (25th October 1854) In the Crimean War, developed from a Russian Attack… Peter ran a finger down the page to the relevant portion. *Lord Raglan sent another message, which the messenger boy wrongly reported to Lord Lucan. Lucan instead of directing the Light Brigade to the causeway, ordered it up a heavily defended valley to the North. Of 673 horsemen, 113 were killed and 134 were wounded, others were taken prisoner. Major William Morgan was awarded the Victoria Cross for saving the life of a private soldier. In so doing he lost his own left arm.*

"Have you found what you were looking for ?"

"Yes, thank you."

"What's it for ? A history class ?"

"No," Peter explained, "an ancestor of mine was at The Battle of Balaclava and won the Victoria Cross."

The librarian smiled with disbelief and moved off to help another boy with a more serious enquiry.

Peter read through it again. *Lord Raglan sent another message, which the messenger boy wrongly reported to Lord Lucan.* Had he been the messenger boy ? Had he been responsible for The Charge of the Light Brigade ? Had he been responsible for one hundred and thirteen deaths and one hundred and thirty-four wounded ? Had he been responsible for William Morgan losing his arm ? Peter was certain that he had been. It was a terrible feeling to have caused so much suffering. But the reports in the book did not quite fit in with what his father had told him or with what he had himself seen just prior to the battle. Things were wrong. He decided to go back and try again to seek the help of his famous ancestor.

COLONEL WILLIAM EDWARD MORGAN VC:
BORN 11TH NOVEMBER 1820 DIED 21ST DECEMBER 1891
That evening he again took out his Grandpa's family tree and began to write. He was learning just a little how to control the pen and travelling back in time was becoming quite an adventure.

"In November 1890 Colonel William Morgan celebrated his seventieth birthday. At the time he was living in retirement with his old friend and batman..."

"Come on in boy if you are coming. Don't just stand there in the doorway making a draught. No need to worry, I won't bite you."

It was definitely William Morgan but not the young officer Peter had met thirty-six years previously. Morgan no longer had a beard about his chin but he had retained a moustache. This, together with his hair, was now quite white and not jet black as it had been before Balaclava. The sleeve of his jacket was limp and pinned neatly to his breast.

"So you are Peter, the grandson of my cook, come to visit ?"

"Yes Sir."

"Fibber !" Colonel Morgan pronounced the work clearly and slowly opening his mouth very wide. The word was kind of harsh but spoken gently. "I know very well who you are Peter Morgan. I know where you have come from, I know when you have come from and I know why you are here."

"Do you Sir ?"

"Yes, I do Peter. Shut the door, come and sit down. Do you want a glass of port ?" Morgan smiled. "No, perhaps you are too young for that. Tell me, just how old are you Peter ?"

"Twelve."

"Is that how old you told them when you enlisted for The Crimea or was it fifteen ?"

"I think it was fifteen Sir."

"You don't have to call me Sir now Peter. Why not call me Grandpa ?"

"But...?"

"I am your Grandpa you know, well sort of at least. Let me see, I am your great-great-great-great-grandfather." He counted off the greats using the fingers of his right hand against the arm of the chair. Peter checked them in his mind. "You are the son of David Morgan the doctor, I wonder what he would have thought about the hospital where they cut this off." He pointed to where his arm should have been and laughed. "Made a good job of it though if you ask me."

"I know all about you Peter, all about your father and your grandfather and that old villain your great-grandfather Richard Morgan. What was it you used to call him – Grandpa Morgan ? Had to write more than a few stories in my day to earn a knighthood, I never got one more's the pity."

"How do you know ?"

"I've been there Peter. I've met them all, all of our family including Pirate Morgan. I was with him when he stole Teach's treasure."

"So was I."

"I know and perhaps your son will be as well, I didn't recognise you at Balaclava I'm afraid. I was a fool in those days, headstrong, but now I know exactly who you are. You know I think you should have that glass of port. Would you like a glass of port ? I think you should."

"Thank you Sir."

"Call me Grandpa, go on try it for size."

"Thank you Grandpa." The words rolled off Peter's tongue with some ease.

The old man fumbled the decanter with one hand and managed to pour a glass of the rich dark liquid. "It'll do you good." Peter gently sipped and was not sure if he liked the taste or not.

"It's the very best Peter, nothing second rate in this house. So what are you going to do with that pen ? You obviously know all about its secrets."

"I don't quite know yet Grandpa."

"I do, I've seen you. You've started to use it already or else you would not be here."

Peter had a hundred questions he wanted to ask but two were of the absolute priority. "Grandpa, was I the messenger boy at Balaclava who gave the wrong message and sent all those men to their deaths ?"

"I do not know the answer to that Peter and if I did I don't know if I should tell you. Some things in life are best left as a mystery. If you read your history books you will learn that the whole Crimean War was made up of mistakes. I was there after all and can confirm them to be correct. All wars are mistakes. Is that a terrible thing for a soldier to say ? The Charge of the Light Brigade was just one of many, many mistakes."

"But was I the boy ?"

"That's all I know and that's all I intend telling you." William Morgan picked up his pipe, slowly filled it one handed with tobacco, lit the bowl and blew out a cloud of smoke. "But that's not the question you came here to ask me is it ?"

"No Grandpa, not exactly."

"Well ?"

Peter wondered how to begin. "The pen, Pirate Morgan stole it…"

"Stole is a hard word and after all these years, removed would be a much better way of putting it."

"Yes."

"Well, there's a boy about to join our school whose name is Christopher Teach."

"Christopher Teach ? Indeed, are you sure ? I think you'll find you have got that wrong."

"No I haven't, he starts in my class tomorrow morning and I have to look after him while he settles into school. I tried to ask Grandpa Morgan what to do and we ended up on…"

"The Titanic," Colonel Morgan interrupted, where you found the first officer was one Winston Teach."

"How do you know ?"

"Because I've been there Peter. And now you find that my oldest friend and personal valet is also called Teach ?"

"Yes, what can I do ? Has Edward Teach followed our family through all generations since the days of Pirate Morgan ?"

"That he has." Morgan blew out another cloud of smoke and chewed on his pipe.

"Then why didn't Grandpa Morgan warn me when he gave me the pen ?"

"Because he never knew."

"But how come ?"

"Because Winston Teach went down with the Titanic. It's part of the deal Peter, if you want the pen then Edward Teach's descendants go with it. Grandpa Morgan never knew about Winston Teach so he could hardly tell you could he ? Each generation of the Morgans must deal with the Teach family in his own way. Me, I've made a firm friend of John Teach, he has become like a brother to me."

"Didn't Bishop Morgan tell Grandpa about the Teaches ?"

"It was all he could do to tell him about the pen."

"So how should I deal with Christopher Teach ?"

"That's another question I cannot answer Peter but be assured you will manage it and manage it in a most unique way I can tell you. Like I said, I have been there and I've seen you. I've met your son Peter and your grandson and your great-grandson. You'll get by, I know you will."

"You've met my children ?" It seems quite incredible .

Morgan blew out a third cloud of smoke. "I have Peter, they will be good people so don't worry. Now stop writing, go home and sort out your relationship with young Teach. Just before you go I want to say how very sorry I am for the way I treated you when we met before at Balaclava I mean. It cost me an arm to learn that other people in the world matter, but now I feel it was an arm well spent."

Peter moved to speak.

"Say nothing Peter, go home. But come back someday and see me, I'd like that. I'll be waiting but now you must go, young Teach is waiting for you."

PETER DAVID MORGAN:
BORN 14TH SEPTEMBER 1980

"Peter Morgan, there you are. I've been looking all over for you."

"I've been working in the library, Mrs Green."

"I am very pleased to hear it Peter even if it is rather out of character for you. Keep it up. Now our new pupil has just arrived and will be starting this afternoon."

Peter felt his pulse rate increase highly and his stomach tighten. "Christopher Teach is here already ?"

"Well not exactly there's been something of a mix up. First of all it's not Christopher, not a boy I mean. Our new pupil is a girl, Christina Teach. Secondly, she's half a day early and I've got to get her sorted out into classes by this afternoon."

The news that it wasn't a boy came as something of a relief but the name was still the same – Teach.

"So you see I won't be needing your help after all Peter. I'll have to ask one of the girls to help her out for the first few days."

"Oh no Mrs Green, I don't mind honestly. Please let me do it, please let me look after her."

"A girl would be better Peter."

"Please Mrs Green."

The wise form tutor with so many years of experience looked at her pupil. Peter Morgan had always been a very polite and sincere boy but one who never pushed himself. He had handed in a couple of rather good pieces of work lately and there he was working in the library during the lunch hour. His father was by all accounts a brilliant doctor and, of course, there was his grandfather but poor Peter never came out as anything more than average. If only he would try harder she was sure he could do much better.

"Go on then Peter." Time was running short, she didn't really have time to find and brief one of the girls."

"Thank you Mrs Green, I'll make a good job I promise."

"I am sure you will. Come along and I will take you to meet Christina."

Christina Teach may have been only twelve years of age but she was stunningly beautiful. Peter, who had never really noticed before, suddenly found himself realising there was such a thing as the opposite sex.

"Peter, this is Christina. Christina, this is Peter."

He did not know what to say so just smiled. It was all rather silly. Christina settled for a shy, "Hello."

"Well don't just stand there Peter, let Christina copy down your timetable. Where's your school diary ?"

During the afternoon Peter became a little less tongue tied and more attracted to Christina. By the end of the last lesson he had all but forgotten her name was Teach. By the time he was on his way home he wondered what it was like to be in love and if it was possible to be in love at the tender age of twelve.

Peter had maths homework that evening and made a special point of not using Grandpa's pen to do it. The work was terribly hard and he knew he must have done most of it wrong.

"Peter," Janet called up the stairs, "telephone."

He was relieved to have any excuse to leave that homework.

"Your girlfriend," she sniggered covering the mouthpiece. "At least it's a girl anyway."

"Peter ?"

"Christina, is that you ?"

"Look Peter, have you done that maths homework yet ?"

"Doing it now."

"I can't understand it and I don't want to make a mess of my very first piece of work in a new school."

"To be honest I don't have a clue about it myself."

"Ask her round," Janet taunted. "I dare you."

"Go away. No, not you, my sister."

"Could you help me ? I mean would you come round and we could work together ? I hope you don't mind me asking you but I don't know anybody else. I've asked my Mum but she's useless."

"If you like." He couldn't believe his own ears. The most stunning girl in year eight had just invited him to her house and he had agreed. What was more her name was TEACH ! "Where do you live ?"

"Lakes Lane, you can't miss the house. It doesn't have a number but it's got a very funny name; Queen Anne's Revenge. I can't think why the people who lived here before us chose such a peculiar, strange name. I expect Mum will change it one day. Peter ? Peter, are you still there ? Peter ?"

He did not answer. He was not there to answer, the receiver lay on its side against the telephone base.

"Peter ? Peter, have we been cut off ?"

Mark Peter Morgan:
Born 17th July 2006
Christina tried the number again but it was permanently engaged. She was sorry, Peter was her only friend in a new school but she did the best she could on her own with the homework.

Peter put his work away and snatched Grandpa Morgan's pen out of its draw. He had used it three times now to go back in time and William Morgan had told him that he had used it to travel forward as well as back. He had also told him that each generation of the Morgan Family had to deal with the Teach Family in their own way. Christina Teach was the generation he would have to deal with but how ? He was frightened a little and what had William Morgan said about his doing it in a most unique way ? What exactly had he meant ? Peter was about to make his first journey into the future and find out. He began to write. *I was born on Sunday 14th September 1980. Next year I will be thirty-five years old and…*

It was working, the sensation now so familiar to Peter came as his mind empties of all the clutter stored by a twelve year old boy to be replace by the information of the year 2015.

"Is Mark at home Mrs Teach-Morgan ?"

"Hello Peter, yes come in."

So Mark was his son. Peter's own son, how peculiar it all felt.

Peter found he knew everything about his friend Mark's father, his own adult self. He was to become a scholar, average Peter Morgan who was never anything worthy of note at school would become a professor in the world's most famous university. He knew Oxford University of course, his father had studied medicine there and Grandpa Morgan had read law, but all hope had been given up that Peter would be able to follow in the family tradition. And yet Peter Morgan would become Professor Morgan of Jesus College, the youngest professor in the modern history of the university. He so very much hoped that his father had lived long enough to be proud of his achievement.

But the name ? The discovery of his own future success had so dulled his mind that he had to let it pass, then it had come crashing back like thunder. What was it he had called Mark's mother ? His own future wife ? Peter's name was of course Morgan, but he hadn't called her that, not Mrs Morgan but Mrs Teach- Morgan ! How could that be ?

Peter knew he was now in the role of a friend of Mark Teach-Morgan and that he had been invited to spend the summer with Mark's family in their Florida holiday villa. Marks father was going to deliver a series of lectures at Miami University's summer school. Mark's mother looked familiar, familiar of course because she was Christina ! It was obvious but totally impossible to comprehend. So would Christina Teach become the wife of Peter Morgan and he two feuding families be united after three and a half centuries ? Was that what William Morgan meant by a unique way of dealing with the Teaches ?

Peter felt content and warm inside but afraid at the same time. As he considered the various possibilities the pen moved on of its own accord. When his mind cleared he was nearly two centuries deeper into the future. He was still in the body of a twelve year old youth and he was still a friend of the Morgan boy but he was now Coady Michael Teach-Morgan, six generations from Mark and his mother Christina.

FLIGHT-CAPTAIN MICHAEL ROSS TEACH-MORGAN
BORN 27TH APRIL 2161

Although Peter knew who he was and where he was he simply could not work out when he was. It was all very confusing, he could not recognise the room. There were no windows and there were no lights yet the room was bright and fresh. In the corner was the familiar Bico unit humming away to itself. Bico ? Whatever was a Bico ? Stupid question. Peter scolded himself, everyone knew what a Bico was. Originally called a biocomputer it was a combination of the old fashioned silicone computer and the more modern biological technology. Peter vaguely recalled that his friend's family had something to do with the founding of the TM Corporation that had developed the original unit.

"Bico," Peter called out, "be so good as to remind me where I am."

"You are onboard the Space Probe Anna, it's long-term mission is to investigate micro laser waves presumed to be emanating from a life form in deep space, possibly located within sector seven of the Galleco Constellation. Would you like me to print out the information for you ?"

"No, that won't be necessary but tell me why am I here ?"

"You and your family are here with your father who is the ship's senior navigator."

"Who is the captain ?"

"Our captain is Flight-Captain Michael Ross Teach-Morgan of The United Nations Space Fleet."

"Does he have a son on board ?"

"His son Coady Michael Teach-Morgan, born 20th June 2191 is on board."

"Does Captain Teach-Morgan have a personal writing programme in his Bico unit ?"

"That is classified information."

Classified information ? Classified, so that must mean it exists. No one classifies things unless they exist, what would be the point ?   The captain of this space probe (How many generations away was he from Pirate Morgan ?) had the pen – Grandpa Morgan's pen. It was in the Bico unit. The union of the Morgans and the Teaches looked to have stood the test of time.

"Bico, can you print me the male line of the Teach-Morgan Family from, say 1980 ?"

"Some of the data is missing from the files but I could reproduce most of it for you."

"Do so please."

The Bico clattered a single sheet of paper. Peter took it and studied the list.

BICO DATA OUTPUT: 009871456. 678201
Date of output: 7th August 2201 Earth Standard Year
Data requested by: Peter Bond
Subject: NON-CLASSIFIED
Family Line of Ship's Captain
DATA INCOMPLETE – FULL RECORDS MISSING FROM
THE BICO FILES

Peter David Morgan:
Born 14th September 1980   Died – data missing from file
Age – data missing from file
Professor of History Jesus College Oxford   Broadcaster and historical presenter

Mark Peter Teach Morgan:
Born 17th July 2006   Died – data missing from file
Age – data missing from file
Computer design engineer

Andrew Mark Teach-Morgan:
Born 16th November 2036   Died 4th December 2105
Age 69
Founder of TM Computer Corporation

Jason Andrew Teach-Morgan:
Born 8th March 2066   Died 14th April 2150
Age 84
Engineer on the first Bico design project with the TM Computer Corporation

Kirk Jason Teach-Morgan:
Born 1st June 2106   Died 30th May 2156

Age 50
Space Anthropologist

Ross Kirk Teach-Morgan:
Born 16th March 2136   Died 1st June 2151
Age 45
Stella Scientist

Michael Ross Teach-Morgan:
Born 7th April 2161
Subject still living
Captain of Deep Space Probe Anna
Data ends 0098746 876 0092

It came as a relief that the missing data concerned his own death. Going into the past was all very well but Peter found the future uncomfortable, or was it perhaps it was a fear of learning about his own future ? The Bico data confirmed he was to become Professor of History at Jesus College Oxford and that his son was indeed called Mark. His grandson would be Andrew and great-grandson James Andrew who would design he first biocomputer within the TM Corporation, a company founded by his grandson. But Peter would certainly be dead himself by then, it was a terrible feeling to know he would be dead and perhaps forgotten. The captain of the space probe would be Peter's great-great-great-great-grandson. It was mind blowing.

Two soft notes chimed from the Bico. "There is a visitor waiting outside your room, shall I let him in ?"

"Who is it ?"

"He says he is a friend."

"Best let him in then." Peter expected it to be Cody or maybe one of the other boys. With a five year deep space mission ahead married officers brought their wives on the voyage with them, those with children had them along as well. It was an unusual way of life but they lived, grew up, went to school, played, ate, slept and did everything else onboard.

The face that came into Peter's room shocked the very fibre of his being. "But how ?" He stammered.

"You and William Morgan are not the only ones to use the pen to travel through time you know."

"But —"

"I'm dead. Is that what you are going to say ?"

"Well – yes."

"So are you. Peter, unless that is you are two hundred and eighteen years old."

Peter stood up and walked across the room. " It is you, isn't it ? It was a hope beyond the reason of hope.

There was no reply, only a smile and a faint tear.

"Well, haven't you got a hug for your old Grandpa then ?"

Peter flung his arms about his most beloved relative and shed huge tears of pure joy. "I don't understand Grandpa."

"Don't question the magic too much Peter, just accept it. I used the pen to wander through time and gather ideas for my books."

"I thought you used then pen to actually write the stories and that's why they became best sellers."

"Right enough, then pen put the words together but I had to come up with the ideas in the first place. Do you remember my novel, Lost in Space ?"

"I've seen the film loads of times, it's on the telly nearly every Christmas."

"Well, this is where the original idea came from, the Deep Space Probe Anna."

"But –"

"Don't question the magic Peter, I've told you." Now what are you going to use the pen for ? Have you decided yet ?"

"I'm going to become a professor of history."

"That's a very sober ambition for one quite so young."

"But history bis exciting. I've already been back to the Crimean War where I met your great-grandfather and to the Titanic where I met," Peter hesitated, "YOU."

"So it was you. I've often wondered about that. Of course at the time I knew nothing about the pen, so it was you who saved my life on the Titanic. My mother was lost you know, they never even found her body."

"I'm sorry Grandpa."

"No need to be, it was a long time ago. More than two hundred and fifty years."

Peter was so very confused, his mind was in the most fearful tangle. While being elated at seeing his much loved Grandpa Morgan again, he couldn't work out how it was all possible.

"Grandpa –"

"Yes."

"I know you said we shouldn't question the magic, but how can we both be here, we can't both have the pen together at the same time I mean."

"Of course we can Peter. I am writing forward from my time and you from your time, it's quite easy really."

"Will we meet again in other times ?"

"I would put money on it."

"But Grandpa, I don't like the future very much, it frightens me what I might find out about myself."

"That's why I removed some of the date from the Bico file."

"You did that ?"

"Yes, didn't I tell you, I am the Bico systems manager on this expedition. Don't question the magic too much Peter. Dream a little. Remember what are dreams are for if not to come true. Now off you go home, there's a certain little girl waiting for you."

Peter did not want to stop writing but the pen gave him no choice. It ceased writing of nuts own accord and he was home again. Home again with his whole wonderful future ahead of him.

THE END

The Wild Adventures Of Di Central Eating

AUTHOR'S NOTE:
I was fifteen years old when The Beatles had a hit with Paperback Writer. I loved that song, its words gave me the ambition to become a paperback writer. Since those teenage years writing had been my hobby, I just love scribbling tales of this, that and the other. Submitting my stories to publishers scribbled rejection slip after rejection slip.

It was not until 1992 that my first story book was accepted, Peter's Magic Fountain Pen which was something I wrote for my son's twelfth birthday, you've just read it. I then sat down and penned a series of adventures for a new character I created, Di Central Eating.

The Wild Adventure Of Di Central Eating
Di's First Fish
Platinum Plated Pitchforks
Pathfinders In Space
Rock And Roll Superstar
Nipper
Football Hooligan
The Great Trolley Race
And Then We Were Three
The Gypsy's Curse

Back in the 1990's I never got my act together to offer the text to a publisher. Now we have Amazon and its amazing publishing house both with Kindle e-books and paperback editions which I am certain the Fab Four would just love.

Although this is a work of fiction each escapade young Di has fun with is based on something from my own childhood. So join Di now and yourself have fun in his wild adventures.

David aka Max

THE WILD ADVENTURE OF DI CENTRAL EATING:
Let me begin by quite clearly explaining that my family is not Welsh.

My mother always claimed that our ancestors originated in France and fled to England at the time of the revolution. That may or may not be true, I don't know, to be honest I have my doubts. But of one thing I am certain and that is not a single drop of Celtic, Welsh blood flows in our veins. Not that I would have any objection to being of that nationality, no none at all, for they are a proud race and their soft, lilting tongue is a joy to listen to. But, sadly the Albons never have been and never will be Welsh so there's an end to it.

Why then is my brother called Di ?

I was just two years old when Brother David came along. Two years old, toddling and full of infant chatter, mispronounced words in a language all of my very own, well I guess I understood what I was on about at least. But my mother could not and try as she did she never managed to teach me to say *David*. In the end she gave up and settled for Di. Even today, within the close circle of the family, Brother David is still known as Di.

But what of Central Eating ?

Now, of course, you all know what central heating is don't you ? Lots of radiators all fed from one boiler keeping the entire house warm. Well something like that anyway. When I was a kid only the very rich had central eating and we weren't even ordinary rich. Every morning, before he went out to work, my father had to light the downstairs coal fire. He would scrunch up the previous day's newspaper, pile a wigwam of kindling wood about it then encircle the construction with lumps of coal. A match gave the initial light which Dad would fan and coax into a roaring blaze. Not that it worked perfectly every time, aborted attempts were common and were followed by the entire process being repeated: the newspapers, the kindling wood and the carefully selected coals. Those fires kept our lounge lovely and warm, with a back boiler heating the kitchen but the rest of the house was as cold as the grave. Di and I used to have competitions to see who could chip the biggest slithers of ice off the bedroom windows where the condensation froze overnight. That was central heating, or the lack of it, but Di was Central Eating. Eating, not heating.

The thing was when Di was about six years old his baby teeth started to fall out. Most children lose their baby, or milk, teeth as a gradual process over a number of years but Di lost four bottom teeth and three upper teeth in the space of a few months. All he had left at the front of his mouth was one stubborn peg that refused to budge. Poor old Di found it quite a handicap trying to eat. Munching at the side of his mouth proved impossible so all he could do was to trap whatever it was with this single, central tooth against his bottom gum. Hence Central Eating. I do not know where this name originated but until well after his mouth filled again with adult teeth David Albon was known to all as Di Central Eating.

Di and I used to attend Banners Gate County Primary School which took all children in the neighbourhood from the age of five years until they left at eleven. Those up to the age of eight were in the infant department while the older ones belonged to the juniors. the infants had their classrooms on the left hand side of the school and the juniors on the right, that was if you stood with your back to the headmistresses office and faced the hall. If you turned round then the infants were on the right and the juniors on the left. I expect you understand. In the middle were all the important parts of the school like the headmistresses room, the secretary's office, the hall, the dining room and, of course, the dreaded school kitchen.

Goodness how I hated school dinners and Di found eating anything near impossible. Thank the Lord we only had to stay one day a week. Like most mums in those days, our mum did not go out to work and was always at home to cook a midday meal for us. But Thursdays were different. Thursday was Young Wives Club at the local church and Mum, being on the committee, had to get things ready for the afternoon meeting with no time to make us lunch.

School dinners weren't exactly bad, they were diabolical consisting of the most fiendish menus. Tapioca pudding, boiled cabbage, swedes, cheese pie and toad in the hole with real live toads ! Of course the cooks were not working at all to prepare meals for the children, nobody thought that, but really for the local pig farmer.

You see after we had eaten our fill, which usually wasn't very much, all the scraps had to be tipped into the pig bin. This was a large metal dustbin, well more than one dustbin on most days, sometimes three on a bad day. At the end of the meal these were wheeled outside to await the pig-man. He came, I think, every other day to take away all the full bins and leave empty ones for the next two days. I expect he had contracts with all the schools and that his pigs grew very fat on it all. Funny to think that when we eat bacon and egg we are really eating recycled cabbage and tapioca pudding. Makes you want to become vegetarian doesn't it.

It was on the day the pig-man came that it happened, it must also have been a Thursday for I remember Di and I were to stop for school dinners. I had just passed into the junior department moving to the right, or was it the left, hand side of the school while Brother Di stayed in the infants on the other side. The juniors and infants had different morning and afternoon playtimes but during the lunch hour had to share the same playground. We older juniors would then try to take no notice of the infants, being careful to keep away from them. It simply was not done to be seen playing with babies now that we were eight years old.

The pig-man always came during the junior playtime, some of us on that day stood and watched as he drove his small pick-up truck across the playground to the back door of the kitchen and the waiting pig bins. First of all he went and checked how many full bins there were. This he did by picking each bin up in turn and judge-weighing the contents. That day all six bins were full, a bumper collection. Very quickly the new clean bins were off-loaded and the full ones humped on to the back of the pick-up truck. Then he was off and we returned to our games.

A sharp blast of the teacher's whistle spelt the end of playtime and we lined up waiting to return to our classrooms. But something was up. Miss Evans, the headmistress, was at the front talking to the teacher on duty. Someone was in for it ! Mis Evans had the habit of talking to teachers while in the presence of children by placing a hand in front of her face and talking out the corner of her mouth. It made it quite impossible for us to hear what she was saying. But it was certain that at least one of us was in big trouble and every child present searched their memories for anything bad they had done over the last few weeks. What terrible discovery had Miss Evans made ?

"Richard Albon would you come with me please."

I looked round in panic. Richard Albon, that was me. Had she said my name or had I heard wrong ? What had I done ? Nothing, no nothing, she hadn't called my name at all. But she had. Miss G M Evans, Headmistress and demi-god of Banners Gate County Primary School was soon marching through the lines of children to collect me. My heart thumped and my legs turned to jelly. I would soon be dead, but what had I done ?

I had never before been inside Miss Evans office. Within an instant I took in every fine detail of the room. In fear I guess I was searching for where she kept her cane. As Miss Evans closed the door behind us I noticed Mrs Lewis was in the room sitting in the corner. Why on earth was she there ? She was Di's teacher. I was soon to find out.

"Have you seen David ?" She asked shakily.

"We walked to school together this morning," I explained. Perhaps it was Di who was in trouble and not me after all. I wondered what he had done and how, as his big brother, I could try to protect him.

"Have you seen him at all since then Richard ?" Miss Evans asked slowly, seating herself behind the big desk that dominated the room.

"No Miss Evans. What's he done ?"

"He's gone missing," Mrs Lewis blurted out. Miss Evans turned and scowled at her. It was evident the interruption was not appreciated.

"You didn't see him while you were out at playtime ?"

"No Miss Evans, he's still in the infants and I'm in the juniors now."

"I know that Richard but when Mrs Lewis took her class back after the infant playtime David wasn't with the other children."

"Perhaps he went to the toilet," I ventured.

"We've searched the toilets and now I've got prefects checking every classroom."

"His friends said he was playing hide and seek," Mrs Lewis spoke again, "and no one could find out where he was hiding."

"Thank you Mrs Lewis," Miss Evans scowled again. "I'll handle this. Do you think he may have gone home Richard ?"

"No, today's Thursday."

"Thursday ?"

"We stay to school dinners on a Thursday."

"But would that stop him from running off home ?"

I thought that school dinners gave the perfect excuse for anyone to run off anywhere but explained that Di could not possibly have gone home because he knew our mother would not be in.

"I think I'll ask the secretary to telephone home just in case," Miss Evans lifted the telephone receiver, placed a hand in front of her face and talked out the corner of her mouth. It must have been a permanent mannerism of hers for I could see no harm in my hearing her ask the school secretary to ring my Mum.

As soon as she had finished speaking there came a knock at the door. It was the prefects reporting back the results of their search. They had failed to locate Di. The secretary then came in to explain there had been no reply on our home telephone.

"Do you know where your mother will be ?"

I explained all about the young wives club, the committee and Mum having to be there early to get things ready.

Miss Evans paused sensing something terrible must have happened. She stood up, placing her hand upon the desk, fingers spread and leaned upon them. "I want one more thorough search of the school and then I'm calling the police."

Of course, the search no matter how thorough, did not find Di.

The police, sniffing a murder, or at the very least a kidnapping descended on the school in force. Mother was collected from the young wives and joined a crisis meeting in Miss Evans's office. I was still there and so was Mrs Lewis now looking very pathetic and nervous. Mum came in having been briefed by the police along the way. When Miss Evans joined us again she had a big policeman with her who was obviously taking charge. He sat himself down in Miss Evans's chair behind Miss Evans's desk and looked at each one of us in turn before speaking.

"My name is Detective Chief Inspector Benton and I will be heading the investigation." He turned to my mother. "Let me assure you Mrs Albon that no effort will be spared to find your son and, God willing, when we do he will be safe and well."

I don't think that my mother started to cry but I do remember she didn't speak as she reached out and took my hand. It made me feel silly and just like a baby. When you are eight years old you do not want your mother to hold your hand do you ?

The policeman continued. "I've got twenty-five men searching outwards from the school and Miss Evans has given me all the essential facts for the moment. Now what I need next is a recent picture of David."

"We can help there," Miss Evans spoke. "We've just has school photographs taken and we've kept a copy of every child's picture for our records. Mrs Lewis could you please go and find the copy of David Albon's photograph."

"Thank you Miss Evans. Now I've got three loudspeaker vans on their way over and when they are here they'll start touring the streets. The press have been informed and an appeal as to his whereabouts will be in all the evening papers."

The phone rang and was quickly answered by Miss Evans. The police may have taken over everything else but it was still her office even if she could not sit in her chair at her desk. Up went the hand and any speaking she did was via the corner of her mouth. She spoke just a few words before addressing all.

"That was David's father, he's on his way from work."

I did not believe anything could possibly have happened to Di. Who would ever want to kidnap him ? I was sure he must have done something stupid and would very soon turn up. Newspapers, police, loudspeaker vans, there would be hell to pay when they did find him. All that trouble and who was actually going to pay for it ?

A special assembly was called for the whole school to help the police find out exactly who had seen him last. Stupid Brother Di, Di Central Eating with the single tooth, what was he up to ?

The remainder of the morning came and went, very soon it was lunch time. Miss Evans offered my mother a school dinner, as if she wasn't suffering enough. Sensibly she refused but all of the police accepted demolishing huge piles of ginger stodge. When my father turned up he thought we should go home but mother refused. She wanted to stay at school and besides the police were watching the house so if Di did turn up they would be there for him."

I think Mum was convinced that Di was dead, it was difficult to tell what Dad was thinking but I knew the police secretly though the same as Mum. But I knew different, I knew nothing was wrong. I could sense everything was perfectly alright. Di wasn't dead, it was all a big fuss about nothing. Far away in the offices of the Evening Mail compositors were preparing the headlines. What would the neighbours say ?

The secretary brought in a letter for Miss Evans to sign. She read it through before scrawling her name at the bottom. It had not been typed on ordinary paper but on one of those old fashioned Roneo stencils ready for duplicating. It was a message to all parents explaining about Di, urging both care of their own children, warning them not to talk to strangers and at the same time appealing for help find the missing boy.

"I'll see that every child gets a copy to take home before the end of school Miss Evans."

"Thank you." Miss Evans voice was starting to sound unsteady.

We then sat for a while in silence. It could not have been for more than a few moments but it felt like an age. Mum looked at Dad and tried to force a smile. Detective Chief Inspector Benton studied the surface of Miss Evans desk and doodled on her pink blotter. Miss Evans wanted to tell him to stop but said nothing. Mrs Lewis sat twisting her hands in her lap and I shuffled my feet on the carpet.

The quiet was shattered by a fierce knock on the door. It burst open without anyone inviting the caller to enter. He stood there with his cap in his hands.

"Found him in one of the bins Missus. Must have been hiding there and fallen asleep. I'd no idea he was there until I tipped out the bins and he tumbled out into one of the troughs. Fair gave the old boar a fright I can tell you. 'Fraid he's in a bit of a mess but seems to be OK otherwise. Sorry about that Missus."

Bit of a mess ? Bit of a mess ? He stank ! Covered in head to foot in the past two days' school dinners he smelt like a decomposing compost heap. Mum started to cry and hugged him to her getting the filth all over her Young Wives Club best dress.

All my Dad could say was, "Better get you home and into the bath."

Miss Evans managed a smile even though Di was dripping all kinds of horrible stuff over her carpet. The secretary had to go round and collect in all of the letters she had given to the children. The police packed up and went away as quickly as they had come, sorry they didn't have a juicy kidnap or murder to get their teeth into.

Talking of teeth, when the paperboy dropped The Evening Mail through our letter box that day there was Brother Di's toothless grin beaming out from the front page. What an idiot ! Hiding in a pig bin ! I swear the stink stayed with him for a week. Above the picture ran the headline:

The Wild Adventure Of Di Central Eating

I guess with the space reserved for a report of a missing child they had to fill it with something. Mum cut out the article and David, to the best of my knowledge, still has it. The Wild Adventure Of Di Central Eating !

DI'S FIRST FISH:
I can't honestly remember when or why I took up the sport of fishing, a more unlikely pastime I cannot imagine. There is nothing in this world today that would induce me to crouch at some water's edge on a damp Saturday morning, a maggot impaled on a hook at the end of a length of nylon line hoping beyond hope that some gullible fish would entangle ins mouth

on my lure. But at the age of nine I obviously thought differently.

Nearly every Saturday morning between the months of June and the following March I could be seen at my favourite spot on the bank of Powel's Pool casting my float after fish. (April and May were months of agony being the closed season for coarse fishing when any trip to the water's edge would have been highly illegal.)

Powel's Pool was a small lake a few miles away from my home and well stocked with perch, chub, roach and dace. It was even said there was the odd pike or two lurking in the depths but they were too cunning for the likes of nine year old school boys. There was one spot in particular I favoured on the lake, a series of three steps that led down to the water. I have no idea why they were there, they were far too small to be use to launch a sailing boat, but they were ideal for our needs.

I had a fine collection of fishing tackle the pride of which was my rod. This was a ten foot split cane model that had once belonged to my grandfather. I never knew him as he died when my own father was a small child, having contracted tuberculosis in the trenches of World War One. My grandmother found the rod in the loft of her house and I was so please when she gave it to me. There was just one problem. It had been a three piece rod and she could only find the bottom two sections. Not to be put off I replaced it with one of my Dad's greenhouse tomato sticks to which I carefully fastened two rings fashioned out of paper clips, bent into circles round a pencil. It worked well enough and landed many an unsuspecting tiddler.

Not that actually catching the fish was all that important. It was the bike ride to the lake, meeting up with friends, showing off one's fishing tackle collection, munching cheese sandwiches with a hand that had only moments before been plunged into a tin of crawling maggots that made up the expedition. Any catch was only secondary, a bonus if you like.

For most of these expeditions my companion was a lad who rejoiced in the name of Tubby-Taylor. Poor kid wasn't even fat but there were two boys in our gang of friends with the surname of Taylor. Something had to be done to make it clear which one you were talking about so one became known as Tubby-Taylor, I don't think he minded very much.

Now, many years later, I can feel a small satisfaction realising how important it was to Di to emulate his brother but when I was nine it was nothing more than a confounded nuisance. Week after week , Saturday after Saturday, he begged me to take him along. He tried to bribe me, he tried to get my mother to force me to take him along and he tried to appeal to my slender better nature but all without success. For most of the season of 1962 I managed to fend him off but then things took a fatal turn.

For Christmas Great Aunt Gladys brought him a fishing rod. Whatever possessed her to do that I cannot imagine. She was a lovely lady, I cared for her deeply, and I had done her no wrong. So why did I merit such a punishment ? Nevertheless there it was on Christmas morning, a two-piece junior anglers rod complete with reel, line, float and a packet of hooks. It would have been mean then, I guess, to refuse him so I reluctantly gave in. I wish now that I hadn't.

First of all Mum wouldn't allow Di to ride his bike to Powel's Pool so Dad had to take us in the car. True enough he didn't stop with us, returning to pick us up four hours later, but who ever heard of going fishing by having a lift in a car ? Tubby-Taylor was good about it and said nothing as we clambered out of Dad's Austin Cambridge. That was a car and a half. It had white walled tyres and a flash of white paint down each side. With a top speed of ninety miles an hour it was a beastie of a motor car. Unfortunately Dad wrote it off in a collision with a Vauxhall Vellox and replaced it with a more sedate Austin Traveller. But that's another story.

Enough about cars, back to fishing. I has been lectured for an age by Mum about what I was and what I was not allowed to let Di do. As if he would ever take any notice of me. It was him that needed telling, not me. We were only to be away for a few hours and usually I had to make do with two rounds of cheese sandwiches but the day Di came along Mum sent us with enough to feed an army. As well as double the amount of sandwiches there was a flask of soup, packets of crisps, chocolate biscuits and a big bag of apples. If we had stopped to eat it all there would never have been any time to fish.

We ground the crisps and mixed the resulting crumble with lumps of bread which we then tossed into the lake for ground bait. Perhaps that was what caused it to happen, I don't know, but if it was then Smiths could have patented the idea and made a fortune out of the alternative use for their crisps.

As I recall, Tubby-Taylor was very kind to Di. He didn't have any brothers and sisters of his own to make a fuss of, wishing he wasn't an only child. Lucky kid, he didn't know he was born, I'd have given him my brother any day of the week. He helped Di unpack his junior angler's kit and put the rod together. It was a two-piece metal affair with a plastic handle and plastic rod rings. The reel, also made of plastic, was a centre pin effort fixed to the rod by stout rubber bands. There could not have been more than a couple of dozen yards of line but the breaking strain was at least twenty-pounds. Goodness knows what the makers expected anyone to catch.

Di carefully selected two fat juicy maggots, pinched them between his fingers then plunged the hook into them. I was never all that keen myself on putting maggots on hooks, always settling for a quick stab and getting it over with. Di, however, took his time and threaded the hook down the bodies until it was totally disguised.

It took four casts before Di successfully landed the maggots in the right part of the lake. Four casts each with Tubby-Taylor standing behind him issuing careful instructions and advice. Casts one and two landed no more than a few feet from the bank with a dull plop into water too shallow even for a minnow. Number three went in the opposite direction landing some twenty feet behind us in the field. But number four was perfect, at least so Tubby-Taylor said. Di looked pleased with himself, his ear to ear grin about his face. Whatever did he think he was going to catch with such a pathetic set up ? Junior angler's kit my left foot !

Thinking back now, some thirty and more years after the event, I don't think I was qualified to make such a comment. I was not, after all, myself the world's greatest fisherman, far from it. Tubby-Taylor. On the other hand, was quite a fair angler seldom failing to fill his keep net but, somehow, I was never so lucky. The fish liked the bait well enough but always managed to nibble the maggot off the hook without snaring itself on the barb.

For that reason on the day Di came along I decided to use a spinner and try for one of the legendary pike in the deep waters of the lake. On the very rare occasions anyone caught one they always had their picture in the local newspaper and I quite fancied having it stuffed and mounted in a case on my bedroom wall.

I had a fixed spool reel and with the weight of a heavy spinner I was able to cast a long way into the lake. I guess I was showing off in front of Di; casting out, reeling in and casting out again. I know I didn't have much hope of bagging a pike but that didn't matter, Di didn't have the slightest chance of bagging anything ! Then it happened.

The squeal was almost deafening. "My float's gone under the water. Look !"

"Strike !" Tubby called, leaving his own rod and moving to stand behind Di.

"Pull the rod up sharply to fix the hook in its mouth. Here, let me show you."

He needn't have bothered for the fish was already firmly on the end and taking line from the reel. "Start to wind him in. Nice and slowly, nice and gently. Keep the line tight so he doesn't tangle but don't rush him just in case you snap the line."

Snap the line ? What did Tubby-Taylor think Di had caught ? A whale ! That line was strong enough to land a pike ! A pike ? Oh no he couldn't have, not a pike. The humiliation. Please not a pike. I wound my line in and stood to watch, my fingers secretly crossed against it being a pike. At least that is why I think I had them crossed. Deep down it may be I was just a little pleased for Di. After all he was my brother and I did care for him even if he was a champion prat.

I need not have worried too much, it wasn't a pike. There was no way Di could have managed to reel in a pike on his own using a plastic centre pin reel. The fish was offering very little resistance, as if it knew its fate. Either that or it was a geriatric of the aquatic world. No doubt it had been through all this many, many times before. The tempting breakfast that turned out to have a hook in it, that hook pushing through its lip, the indignity of being pulled by the mouth through water then up into the air before being disentangled and placed in the prison of a keep net. A couple of hours swimming round and round trying to find a way out of the net until up ended and freed back into the lake. You would think it would have learned from past experiences wouldn't you ?

Perhaps that was why my own catch was always so modest. All the fish in Powel's Pool had been through it before and knew what they must do to avoid at all costs maggots suspended in the water. Perhaps their mothers warned them against it like ours did telling us not to take sweets from strange men. Or perhaps the drowning maggots could communicate with the fish warning, "It's a trap, please don't eat me."

For a short cast it was taking a lot of turns on that plastic reel to pull the fish in but it wasn't fighting and so Di was coping well on his own. Although Tubby-Taylor was there with lots of advice he did not actually have to take a hand himself, safely leaving all the work to Di.

I caught sight of Di's fish as it was pulled through the water. It wasn't a pike. Relief. But then I found myself urging Di on, willing him to land it. Too often I had lost fish myself in the last moments. If the fish was not firmly on the hook it was all too easy for it to escape when the line was slackened as you reached down with your hand to lift it out. If this particular fish knew that dodge it would be the end of the world. If it got away Di would be upset, I would have been mortified. Brother Di was the absolute pest of a little brother but my brother he was and right then I was sharing his pride.

Tubby-Taylor knew the dodge well and was at the water's edge to lift the catch clear and render escape impossible. In a glitter the silver of it came clear of the surface. I need not have worried for this fish knew neither this nor any other dodge. It was a novice and this was its first time.

I don't know if fish have emotions or understand fear. I expect a marine biologist would say not but this fish did. Looking down I could see the fear in its eyes. It looked wildly about itself unable to move anything but its eyes as Tubby-Taylor held it firmly in his right hand. That poor creature was absolutely terrified and I felt sorry for it.

Tubby showed Di how to unfix the hook from its mouth. "Do you want to hold him ?" He asked.

It was a perch. It was about six ounces and five inches long. It wasn't very old, perhaps in its first season and no doubt then thinking that its short life was over. Di stroked it with the back of his forefinger.

"If you want to hold it wet your hands first, a dry human hand is like a red hot poker to a fish. Watch its spikes," Tubby explained, "they can be quite sharp and will stick in you. See how I've got them folded back."

Di nodded.

Suddenly it felt all wrong that it was Tubby-Taylor coaching Di and not me his older brother but what could I do ? "That's a fine fish Di," I said by way of slight compensation.

"Take him and put him in the keep net." Tubby continued. "Gently, that's the way."

Di did as he was instructed.

"I reckon it was that special mix of ground bait we out together," I added. "Think we'd better put some up for next Saturday ?"

Neither Tubby-Taylor nor I caught anything that day, nor for that matter did we the following week. Shortly before it was time for Dad to pick us up we let Di's fish go, free to swim and free to fight another day.

Di never went fishing again and I stopped later that season. Tubby-Taylor moved away when his dad got a new job and somehow it wasn't the same fishing alone. I suppose I could have gone with Di but in one day he had become the expert and I the novice. In a strange way it kind of drew us closer together. The way Tubby had acted towards him made me jealous, he being the big brother that I should have been, the big brother Di expected me to be.

When we got home Di was strangely modest about his victory. Once he had shared a few basic facts with Mum and Dad he never spoke again about the expedition, the catching of his first and his last fish.

PLATINUM PLATED PITCHFORKS:
Brother Di was nothing if he was not gullible, you could get him to almost believe anything. He still believed in the tooth fairy until he was fourteen and as far as I am aware he still writes to Father Christmas every year. It was on a family holiday that I decided to put this credibility to test, to see just how naïve he was, to measure for posterity his innocence.

Every year my father would organise a summer holiday for the family. For two years we went to Weston-Super-Mare in Somerset, another tine we went to Blackpool and on another we went to Bridlington. I remember it rained every day we were at Bridlington. Today when people jet off for Disneyland in Florida or the beaches of the Mediterranean, Bridlington, Blackpool and Weston-Super-Mare sound very dull places but as kids we looked forward to our visits for weeks, if not months, ahead longing for the adventures they held in store.

It was usual for us to rent a caravan and for Mum to do all the cooking just as she did at home. It hardly could have been much of a holiday for her but she would have it no other way. She always as well imagined there would be no shops where we were staying and that her family would devour twice, if not three times, their usual diet while in the fresh air. She, therefore, packed the boot of the car with box after box of provisions. So much so that there was never enough room for the suitcases. These then had to ride on the roof of the car secured to a luggage rack by yards of jute rope. She also insisted we took almost every stitch of clothing we owned just in case. After all you could never trust the British weather.

For this particular holiday Dad decided on something totally different and much more ambitious. No, it wasn't a cruise down the Nile, at nine years of age I did not know where the Nile was, but the next best thing. For a period of seven days Dad had rented a houseboat on the Shropshire Union Canal. We were to drive up the A5 to the Welsh town of Llangollen where the boat was moored. We would then work our way eastward towards Shropshire. It sounded terrific.

Llangollen rests in a valley through which pass the A5 and the A539 trunk roads, the track of the Shrewsbury – Bala, the River Dee and the Shropshire Union Canal. Of course I did not know all that then, it's very easy to set it all down now with a copy of the ordnance survey map by my side as I write. What I did know was that on the canal sat our home for the next week.

Dad had a photograph of her. She was called the *Penowern* but we had no idea what that meant. I tried to find out as I put these notes together but have been unable to discover any reference anywhere to the name. I suspect it to be of Welsh origin but as I have said before my family is not Welsh and so it remains a mystery.

Penowern, bless her rotting hull, was hardly a Nile cruiser. Built at the same time Noah was taking sailing lessons, she was hardly a cruiser even of the Shropshire Union Canal. I think *stig* is the word I am looking for but never mind it was our passport to adventure and it would suit my purpose with Di very well. Very well indeed.

On the first night as we lay in bed I set the seeds. We boys were sleeping in the forward cabin while Mum and Dad were in the rear. Cabin ? More like a cupboard really but there you are.

"Di are you awake ?" It was a silly question. I'd have known well enough if he was asleep for he snored like a pig. It was something to do with his sleeping on his back and having no teeth in his mouth.

"Yeh."

"Do you know what a leprechaun is ?"

"No."

"Well do you know what a gnome is ?"

"Next door has one sitting by the side of their fish pond."

Wat a fool ! If anyone was at the back of the queue when the Good Lord dished out brains then it was Brother Di. "That's just a model stupid. I mean the real thing."

"What is the real thing then ?"

"Every country's got them you know, little people I mean. In Ireland they call them leprechauns and in England they're called gnomes."

"Got off."

I ignored this and continued. "In Denmark they're known as trolls. I don't remember what they are called in France."

"Frogs ?"

Oh the wit, the humour not bad I suppose but however did I cope ?

"In Wales I think they are called Morons."

"I don't believe you. How would you know anyway ?"

"You learn about these things when you get older. We did it in school but you are too young to understand…"

"I'm nearly seven now," he defended.

"I guess you are so perhaps it's about time you started to learn. After all we are in Wales and you never know."

There my explanation was brought to a sudden and rapid halt. With spot on timing Mum came in and gave us a fearful ear bashing for still being awake. As kids she never hit us but she could kill you stone dead at fifty paces with one lash of her tongue. You never went back for second helpings of that I can tell you. Silent we were then until breakfast but I had said all that needed to be said for the time being. The gem of an idea had been set and Di could sleep on it. The next stage of my plan I had already put into action.

Day two of the holiday saw us pull up the moorings, Dad crank up Penowern's aging engine and splutter out of Llangollen. It was a warm sunny day, Dad was at the wheel, Mum was in the kitchen, sorry I mean galley, while Di and I were sitting on deck trailing sticks in the water. I knew it would come, his curiosity would demand it, so I tried to be patient and just waited.

"Richard."

"Yes."

"What's this, do you know ?"

Perfect !

"Where did you get that from ?" I tried to sound excited.

"Found it in my pocket this morning."

"Go on, you never."

"Yes I did."

"You lucky kid. In your pocket ?"

"Yes. Do you know what it is ?"

"Course I do."

"What is it then ?"

"It's a platinum plated pitchfork." How's that for alliteration ? Not bad for someone of my age. "Must have been left by a Moron."

"What's a Moron ?"

I wanted to say "You are," but resisted and instead, "Like I was telling you last night."

"Gnomes and all that stuff ?"

"That's it, you've got it in one !"

Before we left home I had carefully made a number of these so called platinum plated pitchforks. I had taken small twigs, striped the bark and wrapped silver paper round them. It was unlikely they would have fooled a geriatric blind man with a wooden leg but even such a person was infinitely higher on the intelligence scale than my Bother Di.

"What would a Moron want this for ?"

"Di, I really am not sure you are old enough to know yet."

For a small child I was showing patience not typical of my age. I got up and walked back to where Dad was wrestling with the wheel. Penowern had something of a mind of its own. Although general progress was being made in a forward direction it was not in a straight line but weaving one elongated s-shape after another. I'm not sure if it was Dad who couldn't control it or if the rudder was not connected to the wheel, but our voyage was beginning to attract attention from other boat users. Some just laughed, others waved fists and some swore the most terrible oaths. I think Dad was beginning to wish we had gone back to Bridlington even if it did rain there all the time.

Behind us the engine chugged away with an irregular beat, well not a beat actually, more of a thump and a clang. It was so clapped out it was a wonder it turned over at all. Every few minutes it would cough, splutter, falter and recover.

"What's up with the engine Dad ?"

"You tell me. It's full of gremlins, that's all I know."

"What's a gremlin Dad ?" Di had joined us back on the bridge.

"Little men that crawl into machinery and cause sabotage."

"Nice one Dad ! I couldn't have put it better myself. I looked Di in the eye and nodded back to the front of the boat. He got then message.

Safely seated back at the bow, again trailing sticks in the water, I made my next move.

"Wouldn't mention that pitchfork to Dad if I were you."

"Why not ?"

"I keep telling you, you'll have to wait until you are older. Then you'll understand."

"But I'm nearly seven," he protested again.

"So you've told me many times before." I feigned a certain hesitation before continuing, "OK but you must promise to listen carefully."

"I promise."

"Morons," I explained are the little Welsh people. You don't often see them as they're very shy and only come out at night. They live in small tribes along the banks of rivers and canals. Dad calls them gremlins but morons, gremlins they're all the same thing."

"What do they do ?"

"They steal food."

"And sabotage boat engines ?" Di interrupted.

"Rather looks that way doesn't it. You heard yourself Dad say they've been in this boat engine."

"Have they come onboard to nick Mum's cooking then ?"

"Could be." That was an idea to work on.

Di pulled my pitchfork out of his pocket. "What do they use these for ?"

"When they sabotage and break things they use their platinum plated pitchforks by sticking them into whatever it is."

"Cor. They're trying to sabotage my trousers then ?"

Di was hooked, convinced that little men with the unlikely name of Morons were swarming all over Wales once it became dark creating mischief with their platinum plated pitchforks. I told you he was gullible didn't I ? I'd get him.

Shortly after lunch we reached our first lock. What a palaver that turned out to be. First of all the lock gates were closed against us, with the lock water at a higher level, so we had to draw it off before Penowern could be driven in. Dad opened the sluice gates but forgot to close those at the other end. The result was the level in the lock remained the same while all the water did was to flow in at one end and out at the other. By the time anyone realised there were four other boats lined up behind us waiting to use the lock.

Then Penowern refused to approach the lock in a straight line, hitting first one lock gate and then bouncing onto the other. Fierce shouts came from Mum as plates crashed to the floor in the kitchen, or do I mean galley, where she was trying to do the washing up. The gates were quickly closed and the troublesome Penowern captured. The water rose and the folk from the now five boats queuing behind us dashed to open the forward lock gates in order to speed us on our way.

Di and I thought it may perhaps be a good idea to walk along the tow path rather than entrust our lives to Penowern. The only problem was we had to keep stopping in order to let the old tub catch us up. Ambling along I put my hand into my pocket and produced two more platinum plated pitchforks.

"Where did you get those from ?" Di enquired excitedly.

"Found them just before lunch."

"Where ?"

"One by the engine, remember how Dad said there were Gremlins in it, and the other was in the sugar bowl."

"Cor !" The current expression in use today I think is gob-smacked."

"I told you they stole food didn't I ? Well it looks like these Welsh Morons have been nicking Mum's sugar."

"She'll kill 'em if ever she find out."

"Don't tell her then."

Mum and Dad had been bang on cue, almost as if I had briefed them. I hadn't honest, I did not want Di saying anything to them and blowing my plan. On a count of ten Di had reached seven on the gullible scale and was still climbing. I fully intended him to reach ten and the jackpot before the end of the holiday.

Penowern's progress along the Shropshire Union Canal continued to be slow. There were two more locks that day that had to be navigated, each one every bit as bad as the first we had encountered. Although Dad claimed to have mastered the tiller she still wove her way forward like a snake, defying all attempts towards a straight line. The engine sounded like nails being poured into a tin can while a hippopotamus belched through an out of tune mouth organ. I doubt if we managed ten miles all day long.

In the late afternoon we moored up and Mum served dinner. My mum was, and still is, a fantastic cook. In spite of all the adversity she managed a three course meal as if it had been served in a top restaurant. If the Morons had been about they never touched that meal. Enjoying each mouthful we tried to put out of mind the difficulties of the day. Then Dad brought us sharply back to reality.

I very much doubt if I knew then what an aqueduct was and am certain Di hadn't a clue but I dare not speak. I didn't want Di to get on to the subject of gremlins and morons, at least not in front of Mum and Dad. I put a finger to my lips and indicated for him to keep quiet.

We moored at that spot for two nights and did not reach the aqueduct until the day after. It marked the turning pint of the holiday, the point that is where we turned Penowern round and headed back to Llangollen. Let me explain.

The day after Mum's gastronomic extravaganza none of us got up very early. It was food again that woke Di and I. Somehow it is quite impossible to sleep through the small of bacon cooking. We stuffed ourselves then made ready for the assault on the aqueduct. Mum insisted all the washing was safely done before we cast off, she had not forgotten the previous day when we entered, or at least tried to enter, our first lock. Goodness knew what an aqueduct would be able to do !

Once the last plate had been dried and put away Dad went to start the engine. The starter whirred and the engine spluttered but refused to fire. Dad tried a second, a third and then a fourth time but it just didn't want to know. A check of the fuel tank and lines showed all to be well. Another try, still no good. Next check the electrics, they seemed to be OK. The engine was on strike !

It took Dad two hours to strip it down, clean everything and put it all back together again. "Should be fine now," he assured but we simply did not share his confidence I am afraid.

Another turn of the key. The whir of the starter but again nothing more. Out came the tools and everything was stripped down for a second time. Hands were scrubbed, lunch eaten and yet another attempt made. By then Dad was decidedly rattled. This was not the way things had been planned. Next year we would all go back to Bridlington !

"I can't understand it," he muttered. "I've been over everything twice now. This engine's certainly got gremlins in it."

"Gremlins ?"

Gremlins Di or what is it you called them ?"

"Morons Dad but they can't be stopping the engine now."

Damn it he was going to let it all out and I couldn't shut him up. He had his back to me and the way he was talking to Dad it was impossible to get between them.

"Why not ?" I think Dad was desperate and willing to take advice even from a six year old. But he was not as desperate as I was and still I could not catch Di's eye.

"Because I fed them Dad, they won't break the engine because I fed them and now they'll be happy."

"Fed them ? How have you fed them ?"

"I put sugar in the petrol tank Dad."

PATHFINDERS IN SPACE:
When we were kids we stood at the dawn of the space age, little did we know that with the end of the Apollo Programme there would be an about turn and man's exploration of the universe would be no nearer than it had been at the time of the cavemen. But things had once been different. Yuri Gagarin was an international hero, President Kennedy declared the United States would land a man on the moon before the end of the decade and our television screens were filled with constant speculation of space travel.

There were dozens of different programmes: Dan Dare and Flash Gordon, revamped from the generation of our parents. H G Wells First Man In The Moon from two generations even earlier, Doctor Who and one I remember in particular, Pathfinders In Space. This told of a family who were accidentally blasted into outer space visiting the Moon, Mars and Venus before making their way home again. Kids no longer dreamed of being train drivers but set their hearts on becoming astronauts. Things were the same for Di and me. The only thing is we had a real live space rocket in our back garden.

Project Mercury was putting manned American space craft in Earth orbit. Kids' stuff, I had my own eyes set deeper into space. I had a chart on my bedroom wall diagrammatically showing all the planets of the solar system orbiting the Sun. Mercury, Venus, Earth, Mars, Jupiter, Saturn, Uranus, Neptune, Pluto. I knew them all, how many moons each had, how long it took to rotate about its own axis and how long it took to orbit about the Sun. Not that I needed it but there was a little saying to help you remember the order in which they came: *Men Very Easily Make Jugs Serving Useful Numerous Purposes.*

I taught this to Di explaining which planets we would visit in our homemade space rocket. First we would go to Mars, we wouldn't bother with the Moon, and then to Venus where I was convinced we would find life. Venusian little green men which we would tame and bring home to Earth. To a nine year old it was harmless play, make believe, but Di I am afraid took it as gospel.

Our very own space ship was constructed one Saturday morning. First of all I had taken myself down to our local greengrocer and scrounged from its grumpy proprietor, Mr Tom O'Connell, eight of the wooden boxes he had his oranges delivered in. That in itself was a major undertaking, perhaps easier than flying to Mars. O'Connell would only burn the boxes but protest beyond reason about the small boys that tried to beg them to make go-kart trollies not to mention space rockets. Sometimes he charged sixpence a box but would never have dared to charge me, he valued my Mother's custom in his shop far too much for that.

It took Di and I four journeys to and from O'Connell's shop in order to shift the boxes home. Although we lived just round the corner It took over half an hour to complete the task. On the last visit we called into one of the other shops in the small row that made up the local centre, Ken Riley Hardware, where we paid one shilling and nine pence to buy one pound of inch and a half round head nails. Hammer, saw, pliers and screwdriver were secretly borrowed from Dad's tool box and we were set.

We cut the boxes up into planks and then reassembled them into a square, nailing them precariously together using Dad's hammer and the nails we had brought earlier. The description *square* would be generous, rectangle an exaggeration but the four corners did at least add up to three hundred and sixty degrees. The box was big enough for Di and I to sit in and we entered by way of a small trap door constructed in the side. It had a floor but no roof and less like a space rocket it could never have been. It was my idea how to finish off the exterior and make it perfect.

I went to the garden shed and hunted out Di's Indian wigwam. He used to use it when he played cowboys and Indians, it was the perfect shape for a nose cone and just fitted on top of the box. I nailed the bamboo poles and the fabric sides in place. The exterior of the first inter-planetary manned space craft to leave the Earth was complete.

During the afternoon our attentions were turned to the inside. The priority was the floor. As it was, if we attempted to sit down we would very soon have had perforated bottoms from the protruding nails. Mum came up with the answer in an old carpet which when spread over the base covered safely most of the sharp bits. My Meccano construction set was employed building the life support system, propulsion unit and navigation control, the collection of wheels, levers and dials nailed to the orange box walls. It was a hard sacrifice to make but I took down the chart from my bedroom and pinned it up inside the space craft.

We needed supplies, the journey to Mars and Venus would take many days. Di had a packet of Smarties to which I added half a Mars Bar and a packet of custard cream biscuits. Our space suits comprised wellington boots and a pair of swimming goggles. I had an old camera I had paid a shilling for at the school jumble sale, that would be good for taking photographs of any aliens we met.

"We've forgotten something," Di said.

"What ?" I looked round at our collection, it all looked perfectly in order to me.

"A toilet," he explained. "We'll never make it all the way to Venus without needing a wee."

He had a point of course and I wondered what real spacemen did. I suppose those orbiting the Earth were only up there for a few hours but what if they got caught short ? Would Yuri Gagarin have been quite such an international hero if he'd come back with wet pants ? Then it came to me, obvious when you think about it.

"When you are weightless in space Di you don't need the toilet. Your digestion doesn't work the same so it all stays inside you."

"Oh, I see."

Better keep the drinks down though just in case.

Dad came to admire the rocket, full of sarcasm was my Dad. He stood there rubbing his chin. It frightens me now to try and imagine what he was thinking.

"We're off to Mars," Di explained.

"Are you ? Will you be gone before then lawn needs mowing or should I cut round you, difficult with it sitting here on the grass."

"No problem Dad, we've got our first test flight in the morning."

"Good. Be sure to let me know what time you decide to leave, I wouldn't want to miss the take off."

"Have you got any old paint Dad ?" I asked. "The outside looks a bit wrong as it is."

Dad found us two tins, one of green and one of pink. Hardly inter-planetary colours but we spent the rest of the afternoon applying them to Mr O'Connell's orange boxes. With care we lettered *Venusian Expedition* on one of the sides. Dad took a photograph of our efforts and years later I was embarrassed to discover we had spelt it *Venushian Expedishon.* It didn't matter at the time and was much better than having *Outspan Oranges* on the sides !

I have made mention of it before but I feel I must stress again that for me it was all a game, a childhood fantasy, perfectly harmless, but to Di it was an authentic rocket that would actually fly. Perhaps at the tender age of six it didn't matter.

It had been a warm day and the forecast was mild for the night. We didn't have to go to school the next morning being Sunday and it was at tea Mum made the suggestion. I remember we had sardines on toast, small fish that came in flat tins opened with a key that wound a strip of metal off the side to release the lid and expose the head and tailless little fish laying in a sea of tomato sauce. We used to mash the fish onto the toast and pick out the bones before eating. I never did fancy this very much.

"Eat up Richard, you've hardly touched your tea."

"Not very hungry Mum."

"After then work you've done all day. This is a perfect meal for a spaceman."

Funny, I'd never seen Dan Dare or Flash Gordon dining on sardines on toast. In Pathfinders in Space they ate food from tubes that looked a bit like toothpaste.

"That's a shame because I thought you and Di may like to camp out overnight in your space rocket."

Was it worth it ? I guessed it was so tucked into an ample helping of sardines on toast. Camping out in the space rocket, what a prospect, what a chance for our first test flight. My sudden liking for sardines on toast told my mother how very keen I was on her suggestion. Di had more to say on the matter, he prattled on in excitement for an age.

"Oh Mummy can we really camp out tonight in the space rocket ?" He spoke with elation spitting bits of sardine across the room.

"Just don't disturb the neighbours," Dad added, "the way you snore some nights they'll think we are having an earthquake."

There'd be no sleeping that night, we were off into outer space. It was just possible we wouldn't even be back in time for breakfast.

Sleeping bags were unpacked from the upstairs cupboard and laid out on the floor of the space rocket. A torch was found and entrusted to me for safe keeping. Mum, conscious of her ever present concern that we should be well fed, packed a picnic supper. The way she used to feed us as kids it's a wonder we both never grew up to resemble the obese characters one sees in childrens' comics.

Eventually all was set but first there was something very important to do. Saturday evening was Pathfinders In Space on the television and the next adventure to watch. Already dressed in our pyjamas but supplemented with woollen jumpers and a pair of socks each, we sat round that old Murphy black and white television set waiting for the music that would introduce our favourite programme of the week.

That particular episode saw the explorers stranded on a Venusian landscape without water. As it built towards the climax relief came in the form of vegetation that, when broken, had water inside instead of sap.

"Better make sure we take plenty of water with us."

"No problem, Mum's put up a flask of coffee for us."

There was no problem getting us off to bed that night. By eight thirty we were safely tucked up in sleeping bags inside the rocket, the launch count down proceeding steadily. One by one I ran through the pre-launch checks: life support, booster rockets, retro thrusters and artificial gravity. Di was impatient, demanding to known when we would be on our way.

"You can't hurry things," I explained, "do you want to disintegrate into a million particles as we burst through escape velocity just because we failed just because we failed to check one area of the ship ? You can't rush science Di."

At about T-minus one hour twenty I realised that Di was asleep. Too tired or two bored to wait any longer. I think I may only have made it as far as T-minus fifty before I joined him in dreamland.

I don't remember what I dreamed about, that is if I dreamed at all. When I awoke the next day my mind was quite clear and empty but for a short moment I could not figure out where I was.

"Wakey-wakey my two little spacemen, breakfast is twenty minutes away."

"Morning Mum," I stirred slowly, shielding my eyes from the early sun.

If I awoke slowly Di blizzarded his way into conscience. "We're home already ! Boy, what an adventure. I didn't like Mars much did you but Venus was just super. Can we go back there tomorrow ? That Supreme Leader was frightening wasn't he ? Can you remember what his name is ? Wasn't that city strange ? I think I've left my goggles behind, no I haven't here they are in my sleeping bag. Please can we go back tomorrow ? Do you think Mum will let us ? It came out in a gibberish splutter of euphoria that continued on and on and on. He was a real born again fruitcake, my brother.

He hardly came up for air during breakfast and was still confabulating at lunch time. During the afternoon we went to visit our grandmother where he churned it all out again. He honestly thought we had flown about the solar system overnight in a rocket made from a wigwam and Mr O'Connell's orange boxes. I presumed he dreamed it all. I envied him that dream, but to regard it as reality was naive even for a six year old.

Every Sunday we used to visit my grandmother, it was something of a ritual. Some weeks we were invited to stay for tea while on others we left to eat at home. The invitation was a kind of barometer measuring how the old lady felt about our company on each particular visit. With Di chattering away ten to the dozen we certainly weren't offered anything that Sunday afternoon. I don't think my gran had any interest at all in interplanetary travel.

He was still going on about it at bedtime and went to school the next day telling all who would listen about his adventure. Do you remember when you were in the infants how you used to have to stand up on a Monday morning in front of the rest of the class to tell your *news* ? No prizes for guessing what Di's news was. Mrs Lewis told Mum about it at parents' evening a few weeks later saying what a vivid imagination her son had and showing her the story he had written up in his news book: Di Central Eating – Pathfinder In Space and First Man on Venus.

ROCK AND ROLL SUPERSTAR:
We kids grew up in a magical age the like of which had not been seen before and has not been seen since. It was a decade that began with Rock and Roll and ended with Flower

Power. The austerity of the post war era was gone and all were able to look forward to a bright and exciting future. With a little luck, hard work and talent anyone could be transformed from rags to riches.

Talent was a word we were all familiar with, had we not heard the parable of the talents. Talent was a coin, the wise young man in the story had been given five, or was it ten, talents and had made ten more. The fool had been given just one and he had buried it in the ground. It was confusing, therefore, when we saw a poster in the library window advertising a talent competition, did it mean they were going to hand out talents and that we had to go out and make more before some predetermined day of judgement ? I thought to myself I wanted nothing to do with that.

Next day in school assembly the headmistress, Miss Evans, started to talk about the contest and very soon I realised it had absolutely nothing at all to do with the Biblical talents. This had something to do with singing, dancing and telling jokes. I had about as much interest in that as I did in the parable at Sunday School. I kind of stopped listening but I do remember something about local heats before a city final and the first prize being a family holiday to Butlins. Entry forms could be collected from the secretary's office during morning playtime.

Butlins, everybody wanted to go to Butlins but I was rather surprised to learn that our headmistress, the revered Miss G M Evans had never heard of Butlins Holiday Camps.

At the end of World War Two along came Billy Butlin who brought up some disused army camp or other, bunged in the odd swimming pool, imported a load of holiday-makers, laid on dawn to dusk complementary entertainment and becoming a multi-millionaire in the process. Every child wanted to go to Butlins but somehow it wasn't exactly our Mum and Dad's scene. Something I once remember being said included not touching it with a disinfected bargepole. Although I let most of Miss Evans assembly pass over my head I think it was the prospect of time at a holiday camp that made Di prick up his ears. After school that day he brought home an entry form.

The competition was being organised by the town council with heats in each of its local areas. The finals were to be held in the town hall with a first prize of a family holiday for four at a Butlins Holliday Camp of the winner's choice.

"Well what could you do ?" Dad asked later peering over the top of the evening paper.

"I'm going to sing."

"Can you sing ?"

"'Course I can sing, when I grow up I am going to be a rock and roll megastar."

"If Richard were to sing with you it could be a duet like the Everly Brothers." Thank you Mum I did not need any suggestions like that one.

"More like the Beverley Sisters," Dad added.

"There's three of them, The Beverley Sisters," Mum defended, "and I for one am proud that Di wants to enter."

"Better not win though 'cos I'm not going to Butlins." That was fine, if Di won we'd go without him.

"What are you going to sing ?"

"Wooden Heart by Elvis Presley."

Now my mother fancied herself as something of a musician, she had piano lessons when she was a child, so took on coaching of her son in the Banners Gate heat of the Royal Sutton Coldfield Children's Talent Contest. We had an old piano in our front room and every afternoon after school Di would practice while Mum plonked away on the keys. He could not have sounded less like Elvis Presley and I'm sure Elvis had never heard of the songs Di elected to sing.

It could be that was a bit unfair, somehow I do not think Di chose the songs himself but rather had them chosen for him by Mum. She turned him right off Wooden Heart and refused anything by Cliff Richard who she regarded as some here today and gone tomorrow pop artist who would never last.

Entrants in the singing section of the contest had to select two songs and very soon the house filled with those Di was to sing. You know what it is like when you can't get a tune out of your head, maddening ! Well that's how it became for us. One day I even caught Dad whistling one of them in the bathroom while shaving before work.

Mum had gone along to Curtis Music and Record Store and ordered manuscript copies of the songs. As I write now those wretched words and their accompanying melodies are starting to invade my brain again. If I can't get to sleep tonight for hearing them I'll… !

It was strange all the effort Mum was putting into preparing Di for the contest, almost as if she wanted him to win and for us all to go off to the dreaded Butlins. Even Dad was tolerant but then I guess they both knew Brother Di didn't stand a chance.

Then one week-end Dad flipped and went over the top. When he came home from work on Friday he had with him what looked like a small suitcase. When the lid was opened an old fashioned wheel to wheel tape recorder was revealed.

Such an item of equipment was a major status symbol for many families and needless to say we did not own one. At first I thought Dad had gone out and blown goodness knows how much money on it but then he explained that it was only borrowed from a friend at work. Di was about to make his first recording.

The microphone was set up on a stool by the piano, Di positioned about two feet away from it then Mum began to play. Dad was an absolute novice and there was no such thing as automatic recording levels on machines in those days. It took six attempts to get it right and even then the piano sounded hollow and distant while Di's voice was too full of treble pipes and tinny. But never mind, the recording was made although none of us had any use for it beyond that week-end, after all we did not have a tape records of our own to listen to it on.

As time for the contest drew nearer Mum took Di down to the Co-op and brought him a special outfit to wear. Blue trousers, a red checked shirt and a yellow bow tie. He looked a right idiot I can tell you and I was glad I wouldn't have to watch him perform but I'd got that wrong. We were all going, no choice in the matter. Mum had got tickets for us all and for Gran and for Great-Aunt Gladys as well. How totally embarrassing !

The preliminary heat was not to be in the town hall but at the local secondary school. We arrived early in order to get seats near the front. Dad went and brought programmes for us all. There was Di's name together with the titles of the two songs he would be singing. He wasn't in the least bit nervous and didn't seem to realise what he was letting himself in for.

The first contestants were dreadful, a brother and sister duet. The brother played the violin and the girl a recorder. Neither were in tune and the relief on their faces when the end came was pathetic to see. The next entry was an older boy who tried to impersonate Arthur Askey. His opening line of *Hello Playmates* was the funniest thing he said during his entire act. At the end the audience politely clapped.

Di was next. Full of confidence he swaggered up onto the platform, pulled himself up to his full three feet six and a half inches then smiled. That brought a titter from one corner of the hall and I pushed myself down into my chair hoping no one would realise he was my brother.

The pianist struck up the chords of the introduction, Di drew breath then launched into his first song:

"All I want for Christmas is me two front teeth, me two front teeth, yes me two front teeth."

"All I want for Christmas is me two front teeth, yes me two front teeth, so I can wish you Merry Christmas."

Even though Christmas was still several months away there were roars of laughter from everyone in the hall, great guffaws of belly-rocking hilarity. Great-Aunt Gladys had to open her bag, take out a handkerchief and wipe away a tear. When Di had finished he took a step forward and bowed. The applause was deafening what with clapping, cheers and even the odd whistle. It went on so long he couldn't begin his second song.

When eventually silence descended Di's timing was again perfect, Mum had trained him well. He put his hands deep into his pockets, pulled out two tooth brushes, held them up then grinned his toothless grin. Again the audience erupted and again he had to wait for quiet.

"You're a pink toothbrush, I'm a blue toothbrush will you marry me some day ?"

There were another seven contestants but none stood any chance. Di was the obvious winner. When the judges confirmed it he had go on stage again for an encore. That family holiday at Butlins was ours for the taking. After such a performance the finals in the town hall would be a walk over.

We were all very proud of Di, even I have to confess that, and I think Dad had forgotten all about his fear of Butlins Holiday Camps. On the way home we had fish and chips with a portion of scraps, all those crunchy bits of batter skimmed off the top of the fryer. Lovely.

Di had to wait four months until the finals. During that time the practices with Mum continued and confidence grew. Victory was certain. Not only did Gran and Great-Aunt Gladys come along again but when we took our seats we saw both Miss Evans and Di's teacher Mrs Lewis on the other side of the hall. So many people.

So many people to watch a victory. So many people to watch a victory that never happened. Di wasn't even placed in the top three. This time there were no wild cheers or shouts of *more – more,* just affable clapping. The first place and the holiday at Butlins went to a girl with pigtails and a brace who played the flute. How could anyone play the flute wearing a brace ? What had gone wrong ? You see there were four months, seventeen long weeks, between Di's victory in the heats and his singing again in the finals. Four months during which Di's teeth grown and filled the front of his mouth. Without a toothless smile *All I want for Christmas is my two front teeth* just was not funny. Poor old Di, no longer Central Eating.

NIPPER:

It seemed to me that Di had been nearly seven for years. If anyone asked him how old he was he would never say "Six" but always "Nearly seven". When it became apparent that he would actually make it to his seventh birthday and that it was only a couple of weeks away Mum, Dad and I put our minds together to decide what to buy for him. Mum suggested he should read more and that we could give him a set of books. Not a good idea. Offering Di a book would have been like serving bacon sandwiches to the Rabbi at a Bar-Mitzvah.

Let me digress for a brief moment and talk a little about this reading business. Although we decided not to buy Di a book for his birthday it does tie up with what we did finally get him. When I first started to learn to read and write in the infant department of Banners Gate County Primary School I began with a little reader called *Nip and Fluff*. Nip was a dog and Fluff was a cat. The book told in the simplest words of their adventures. I can remember almost every word.

Here is Nip.
Here is Fluff.
Nip is a dog.
Fluff is a cat.
Nip and Fluff are playing.
Nip and Fluff are playing in the garden.

And so it went on. One short sentence on each page with a line drawing to demonstrate whatever the canine/feline duo were up to. Goodness who thought up such gibberish but countless thousands of copies were sold ensuring his fortune. Mum bought one of those copies making me read from it to her every night. When it came time for Di to start school Nip and Fluff were waiting for him and the whole process started over again.

Well enough of that, back to the plan for Di's seventh birthday. The most popular toy in the shops at that time was a Dan Dare Radio Station, a pretend toy transmitter-receiver, but it was priced at over five pounds which was well beyond Dad's intended budget. So that idea was relegated to join Mum's collection of books. Di wasn't really old enough for a train set and he used my Meccano set so they were both out as well. With three days left to go still no decision had been made. With so little time left Dad came up with the perfect idea but it was one that would involve us all far beyond Di's seventh birthday.

Looking back I am more than pleased with the decision we all came to that evening as we plotted away while Di was asleep in bed. I wonder, however, if we honestly knew what we were up to. I say *we* to include Mum, Dad and myself but I should explain I was only a very junior partner and doubt if my vote counted for all that much, if anything at all. Now that was unfair seeing how much future responsibility was to fall upon me.

Di's seventh birthday present wasn't just for him, it was kind of for all of us. Dad picked it up the day before, hiding it in Gran's house overnight. He left well before breakfast to collect it in time for Di getting out of bed. With Di being as excited as he was at the prospect of finally reaching the magic age of seven that had to be pretty early.

When Di awoke on the dawn of his seventh birthday the gift was there waiting on his bed. Perhaps it would be better to say that it was the gift that woke him up. It wet all over his bed cover. Can I drop all this *it* stuff now ? It was a HE, Di's present was a puppy dog. A puppy dog the spitting image of the celebrated Nip in the Nip and Fluff kindergarten best seller.

Di's yell of delight could be heard three streets away, it scared the little dog silly and he tinkled all over the bed for a second time. Mum was not amused and Di had to begin his birthday with a bath.

The incontinent pooch was lucky not to be out on its ear right there and then. Mum had to strip and wash all the bedding with no automatic washing machine back in those days. Of course we all called him Nip but within a couple of days it had been extended to Nipper. For the next thirteen years that dog was at the centre of our lives. Wherever we went he went as well, decked in a white ribbon he even came to my wedding. But all that came much later and not until after a lot of water had passed under the proverbial bridge.

While he may have survived that first morning and the wetting of Di's bed there were doubts if he would make it very much further, In anticipation of his joining our little family Mum had laid in a store of tinned dog food. There were several varieties but on that first day he stubbornly refused to eat a thing. Neither would he drink anything that was offered.

"There must be something wrong with him," Mum observed.

"Perhaps he just isn't hungry."

"But he must be," Di pushed a finger into the gooey splodge and offered it up to Nipper. He turned away. "Go on, you must eat something," he insisted, shoving the finger into the animal's mouth. Nipper, true to his name, nipped Di's finger then proceeded to spit out the food all over the kitchen floor. I don't know if you have ever seen a dog spit, it's more like a sneeze, but it spread a small finger of dog food a very long way. The washing of the bed clothes then had to stop to enable the washing of the kitchen floor. It was washed a second time when Di trod in the saucer of milk put down to tempt Nipper.

By lunch time Mum was thinking a visit to the vet may be a good idea. I never was certain if it was to discuss the animal's diet or to have the troublesome creature put down. It was Gran who saved the day.

Di had a birthday tea that afternoon. As well as all his friends both Gran and Great-Aunt Gladys came along to join in the fun. Once he had been shown off Nipper was relegated to the kitchen while the wrapping paper was furiously torn from the packages brought by his many friends. He was kept well out of the way when the jelly and blancmange hit the table. Over the washing up Mum discussed the animal's future with her mother-in-law.

"I am worried about him, I just can't get him to eat a thing."

Gran picked him up, cuddled him and kissed the top of his head. Nipper responded looking into her face. A bond was established that was to last for the rest of his life.

"Richard, get me a slice of bread and butter would you please."

I was there helping with the washing of the jelly plates and sweeping up of cake crumbs. As well as being able to avoid the hilarity of a seven year old's party games in the front room there was also the chance to nick the odd chocolate biscuit that Di and his fellow gannets had missed. There were plenty of sandwiches left which Mum was packing up for Dad's lunches next week. I took one of them and peeled the top slice of bread away from the corned beef below and offered it to Gran.

"Cut it up into little squares will you please Richard."

I did as I was told.

"Now you're going to have some birthday tea as well like a good little doggie. Yes you are, yes you are." She cooed away into Nipper's ear. "You don't want to have to go to the nasty old vet do you ? You want to grow up to be a nice strong doggie don't you." Yuk what soppy talk !

Nipper never did grow much bigger changing little from his puppy days, the canine equivalent of Peter Pan, but that day my Grandmother sorted out once and for all his refusal to eat. She offered up one small square of bread and butter. Nipper sniffed it, cautiously then took it from Gran's fingers and bolted it whole. His eyes looked about for a second bite. It went down whole in just the same way as the first. Then a third, a fourth, a fifth and a sixth until it was all gone. I pulled a second slice from the sandwich, that week Dad had several sandwiches in his lunches with only one slice of bread, and cut it up as before. When Nipper had eaten his fill it was all washed down with a saucer of milk.

Mum's emotions were mixed, she was pleased of course that Di's birthday present wasn't going to pop its clogs before the day was out but didn't enthuse at being shown up by her mother-in-law. "You obviously weren't doing it properly my dear," she had said. I don't think Mum ever forgave Nipper.

Nipper was supposed to be a Cairn Terrier, as I have already explained he never grew to his full size, but looking at pictures of the breed I cannot easily recognise him. He had the funniest face I have ever seen on an animal, not a trace of symmetry anywhere, his left ear pricked up with the right folded over and flopping as he walked. Pointed snout ending in a little black nose and white whiskers. Coat of a dozen shades of brown together with streaks of white. His tail ended as a short stub which when wagged looked as if it would shake off his bottom entirely. All in all, he was quite a deformed little mutt.

When he first joined our little family everybody wanted to take him off for walkies, in fact it is a wonder his legs weren't worn down to the knees. But as the years went by we were never quite so keen. Fortunately we had a large garden so all that had to be done when we were feeling lazy was to open the back door and Nipper could go out and satisfy the call of nature whenever he felt so inclined. Dad used to huff about the little messages he left behind but then he knew where the lead hung on the back of the kitchen door just as well as anyone.

Nipper, of course, also knew exactly where the lead was kept. He would jump and worry away at it. He could never manager to pull it down. In time scratches appeared alongside, they were painted over and reappeared many times. In all those years Nipper never managed to pull the lead off the hook but it became something of a ritual.

The lead business wasn't the only ritual old Nipper developed over the years. There was the cheese. This took place each and every night. Without fail at eight o'clock. Or there about, Nipper would lay on the floor resting his head on Dad's foot. For the next hour he would refuse to budge. If Dad ever attempted to get out of his chair Nipper would clutch his trouser bottom in his teeth and drag behind him. At nine o'clock Dad would say, "Oh well you boys, time for bed." That was the signal. Nipper would sit up and wait. Dad would go to the kitchen, cut two small slices of cheese and that was Nipper's supper. It was absolutely impossible to get away without giving him supper. No way !

Now this was fine when Di and I were little but as we became older our bedtime got later and Nipper's biological clock just could not compensate. So right up until the time I left home I was always told to go off to bed promptly at nine o'clock.

Di's seventh birthday present certainly changed our lives although not the way they were to unexpectedly change when someone else came to live with us. But that's another story and one I'll tell you later. For his eighth birthday Di got that Dan Dare Radio Station. It was his pride and joy for all of a week, was then relegated to the bedroom cupboard and ended up at the church jumble sale.

It was a jumble sale that made me think of Old Nipper who sadly left us for Doggie Heaven many years ago now. I was sorting through some old junk my wife is always threatening to bin when I came across that book: Nip and Fluff. Here is Nip. *Nip is a dog.* I read through it silently from cover to cover, twice. I am not ashamed to admit it brought a tear to my eye.

FOOTBALL HOOLIGAN:
I'm a knock-kneed chicken. I'm a bow-legged hen,
Aint had a fight since I don't know when.
I walk with a wiggle and a giggle and a squawk.
I am a Holt End boot boy !

Guide us through the First Division,
Lead us through the dangerous way.
Let us triumph o're Man United,
Lead us to the Tottenham fray.
Aston Villa, Aston Villa,
We'll support you ever more.
We'll support you ever more.

Easy ! Easy !

"Give it a rest Di !"

Where's your father ?
Where's your father ?
Where's your father referee ?
Ain't got one,
Aint got one,
You're a ….

"Enough Di !"

The goalie is a puff,
The goalie is a puff.
Ee aye addio,
The goalie is a puff !

Do you think you could just possibly guess that Di was a football supporter ? Well if you call supporting Aston Villa supporting football that is. Aston Vanilla, the team everybody licks ! It was the unlikely person of Gran who started it all off.

Before you start imagining a white haired old lady on the terraces, football rattle in hand and scarf about her neck it wasn't like that at all. I doubt if my Gran had ever been to a football game in her life, not even in the distant days of her youth but then she was the world's greatest expert on the football pools. Everything stopped in her house on a Saturday afternoon when the classified results came on the television. It was one Saturday when Mum and Dad were to be out late so Di, Nipper and I were sleeping at Grans.

At about five to five she demanded absolute silence, put her reading glasses on and sat, pen in hand, in front of the TV with a strange sheet of paper.

"What's that for Gran ?"

"Tell you later Di now be quiet it's nearly time."

Time for what Gran ?"

"Quiet Di."

"But.."

"Di, be quiet !"

Blackburn Rovers 2	Arenal 1
Birmingham City 0	Nottingham Forrest 1
Luton Town 3	Crystal Palace 2
Oxford United 2	Aston Villa 2
Tottenham Hotspurs 3	Derby County 0
Norwich City 0	Manchester United 2
Liverpool 3	Leyton Orient 1
Manchester City 2	Newcastle 2
Stoke City 1	Everton 3

And so it went on. We sat in reticence while Gran scribbled the results on the copy coupon of her football pools. It was like a religion to her. Monday morning she would take the week's forecast to the post office, buy a postal order and send the lot off to Littlewoods. She never won a big dividend but over the season she always managed several small pay outs making it a reasonably profitable hobby for her. I do remember that week she won fifteen shillings.

Shillings ? Of course some of you won't know what shillings were. You see once upon a time we used to have a different sort of money in this country to that we have today. The pound was still the same although it was a pound note then and not the silly brass coin we all have today. There were twenty shillings in each pound, a shilling being worth five of today's pence, and twelve pennies in a shilling. So a - penny in those days was worth, now let me see – twelve pennies in a shilling times twenty shillings to the pound equals two hundred and forty which means by modern reckoning and old penny was worth ? Hang on I need a calculator. Point four-one-six-six-six-six-six-six-six P. There was also the half-penny coin, pronounced ha-pen-ey, which would have been worth point two-five- three-three-three-three-three-three-three P. Although they had gone out of use by the time I was born there used to be a farthing, or quarter of a penny which would have been worth – Oh you work it out !

Confused ? Then just hang on a minute longer will you. There were four crowns to the pound and eight half-crowns, each crown worth five shillings and each half-crown worth two shillings and six pence. In silly money today that is twelve and a half pee ! A florin was two shillings or ten pee ! A shilling was known as a *bob* and a six penny piece a *tanner* or a *kick*. So two and a kick or two shillings and six pence or in today's silly money twelve and a half pee. A Guinee was one pound one shilling, one pound ten pee. It was the posh people who used Guinees.

Now what has all that got to do with winning the football pools ? Not a lot but at least you've learned something from English history. Don't ask me what good it will be to you but that's not my problem is it !

Back to Gran's football pool divi. Fifteen shillings, or twenty five pee, was worth something in those days before a succession of incompetent governments invented inflation. Once the results were over Di began to quiz her on the subject of football.

You may think that a young boy should not have been ignorant of our national game but at Banners Gate County

Primary School there were only two men teachers, women couldn't possibly teach football it would have been unthinkable. Mr Lloyd was a cricketer and Mr Sullivan, *Sulligogs*, the deputy head had far more important things to do than teach small boys how to chase a ball about a games field. Di's education was about to be completed.

Part of Gran's winnings were set aside and Uncle George, Great Aunt Glady's unmarried son, was detailed off to take Di to Villa Park the next Saturday. In those days Villa Park had a capacity of eighty-two thousand. I have been there with that number – what an atmosphere, and it was anticipated a near capacity crowd would be in attendance for the local derby against Birmingham City. Gran had the game down as a home win, it was up to Di and Uncle George to see they did not let her down.

Uncle George called round for Di at mid-day. I don't know what had come over me but I decided I wanted to go as well, so we all walked down the road to catch the 29A corporation 'bus which stopped at the bottom of Trinity Road. It was just over a mile to walk from the 'bus stop to the ground, the entire distance was a river of claret and blue flowing towards Villa Park. The police were directing the Birmingham fans in from Wittan Road so not a blue and white scarf in sight. The air was full of chants: *Villa, Villa, Villa !*

Uncle George usually stood behind the goal in the massive Holt End but Gran insisted he didn't take we children into the crush. The Wittan End was reserved for away supporters and old men so we were going into the Trinity Road stand where we found spaces on the half way line adjacent to the trainer's bench and just below the directors' box. We took up our places nearly two hours before kick-off but already the ground was filling quickly.

BBC outside broadcast vans and camera crews indicated the game would be the match that evening on television. Loudspeakers boomed out the latest pop music but were drowned by the singing of the crowd. Some of their word were, well, downright rude and Di memorised every line.

In less than the preceding week Mum had managed to knit us both scarfs in the famous claret and blue Villa colours. We held them out between our outstretched arms and swayed in time to the singing. Occasional chants were heard from the opposing fans but they were soon shouted down, out and into oblivion.

Gran's pool win did not stretch to programmes but Uncle George generously put his hand in his pocket and forked out for us to have a copy each. Di was as happy as a dog with four lampposts.

The pre match noise of the crowd doubled, no trebled, as the teams ran out onto the pitch. Beneath cheers of *Villa, Villa* I do not see how ever they heard the referee's whistle order for the start of play.

After so many years I cannot honestly remember all that much detail of the actual match and want to take care not to drift off into a work of fiction. I haven't a clue who scored the goals but do clearly remember by half-time the noise of the Villa supporters had died away somewhat. To compensate the Birmingham fans had discovered their voices. With a score line of Aston Villa 1 Birmingham City 3 it was hardly surprising. Half-time was an air of doom and gloom. Uncle George hardly said a word, heaven help the people at work next Monday morning, he would be unbearable and Great-Aunt Gladys was in for a bad week-end.

The manager must have given the team a terrible talking to back in the dressing room, they pulled back a goal direct from the kick off.

Aston Villa 2 Birmingham City 3

The crowd decided it was about time it spoke up again.

Aston Villa, Aston Villa
We'll support you ever more
We'll support you ever more

The Birmingham fans were having none of that so countered with:

City ! City ! City !

The equaliser came about ten minutes from full time and was followed by the fiercest battle imaginable.

Aston Villa 3 Birmingham City 3

I wasn't paying that much attention at the time, I guess I was thinking about going home, but the call of "Penalty !" and the sheer ecstatic delight when the referee agreed brought me right back into the game.

Villa lined up for the shot. We heard the manager shout from the trainer's bench, "Chico take it." Chico Hamilton was standing just a few yards away from us waiting out on the wing.

"Go to it Chico," Di called, "you show em ! I've got my fingers crossed for you." Chico Hamilton turned and looked at Di, gave him the thumbs up then trotted to the penalty spot. "Good luck," Di screamed after him.

"He'll need it," Uncle George said joining Di in crossing his own fingers. "By my watch it's full time."

A hush descended over Villa Park, every Villa fan praying that Chico wouldn't miss and every City fan praying he would. They may have lost the two goal lead but a draw away at Villa Park would still be a triumph.

Chico Hamilton placed the ball, looked back again in our direction and waved, paced his run up, drew breath and moved in. Just before the kick he kind of shuffled a half-step and whacked a left footed shot into the back of the net. It cannoned past the poor City keeper who, anticipating a right footed attack, dived totally in the wrong direction. He had hardly picked himself up to face the humiliation when the final whistle blew.

The crowd took up with: *Chico – Chico – Chico.* His fellow players mobbed him but he was pushing his way towards the crowd where we were standing.

"Where's my lucky mascot ?" He called looking at Di.

"Me ?" Di shouted in reply.

"You fellows pass him down," Chico ordered.

Di was lifted high and passed over the heads of the crowd until he was set down on the pitch. In those days, of course, there were no fences, just a low wall between supporters and the pitch. Chico swung Di high onto his shoulders before running a lap of honour with him bouncing up and down and waving as if he was royalty. The crowd loved it. So did the TV producer who had the cameras pan round after them.

Uncle George began to chant. "We're going to win the league, we're going to win the league. Ey-ay-addio, we're going to win the league."

"That's my nephew out there you know."

Those about him took up the call and passed it on to others until every Aston Villa fan in the entire stadium was cheering. "We're going to win the league, we're going to win the league. Ey-ay-addio, we're going to win the league."

Villa didn't win the league that season, it was another twenty odd years before they did, but right there and then, thanks to Chico Hamilton and my Brother Di, Aston Villa was totally invincible.

"Would the parents of the young supporter on Chico Hamilton's shoulders please pick him up from the player's dressing room once the team has left the pitch," the tannoy barked out.

Well how about that !

When eventually we managed to find our way to the dressing rooms and persuade the stewards that we had permission to pick up Di the players were in the bath. The room was a fog of steam from the communal bath.

"Richard, Uncle George over here."

Di was in the bath with the entire team, every one of them modestly wearing a pair of swimming trunks. Where did they find a pair small enough to fit Di ?

"What on earth are you doing in there ?" I asked. "Mum will kill you."

"I'm with my friends."

Chico Hamilton waded across the pool to Uncle George. Her reached out and pumped him with a sopping wet handshake. "I was so scared when the Boss shouted for me to take the penalty and then this young man called after me giving me just the confidence I needed."

"We showed 'em Chico didn't we ?"

"We certainly did my young friend. We saved the game and the honour of the best football team in the city."

Uncle George was kind of proud but felt awkward crashing into the privacy of the dressing room, least ways before any of them could put on clothes other than claret and blue swimming trunks.

"I think we'd best be off and out of your way, there'll be massive queues for the 'buses."

"No, let me give you a lift," Chico insisted. "It's the least I can do, I owe you. Here you dry him off while I get ready. He lifted Di dripping water and offered him to Uncle George. "You can use one of the club towels over there. I don't know where he put his clothes but they are about somewhere."

We all got to ride home in Chico Hamilton's car. I expected it to be a Jaguar at the very least but it turned out to be a mini ! Actually a blue and white mini. He dropped us off at Gran's house where Uncle George had left his car. Gran complained that we didn't have money to waste coming home by taxi.

"But he is one of the footballers," Di protested. He told her all about the game, about Chico Hamilton, about the penalty, about the victory lap and about the communal bath.

"Sounds disgusting to me," she replied. "You'd think a club the size of Aston Villa would be able to afford separate baths for its players ! I shall mark them down for losing on next week's pools coupon."

THE GREAT TROLLEY RACE:

I was one of the best trolley riders at Banners Gate County Primary School and had dreams of following in the footsteps of Stirling Moss or Mike Hawthorn. My arch rival trolley rider was my best friend Jim, some days I would win the race while on others Jim was the victor. About as much effort went into arguing who was the best as did go into the actual races. Our heated discussions extended far beyond mere wooden trolleys with pram wheels and onto anything at all to do with motorised transport.

"My Dad's got a better car than your Dad's got !"

"Well my Dad's a better driver than your Dad !"

"The just you wait until I am old enough to drive,"

It wasn't all that long since the first motorway in the country had opened, The M1. We planned that for a day this new stretch of road would be closed to all traffic, Jim would take his Dad's car and would take my Dad's, we'd then race all the way to London and back. That would prove once and for all who was the best trolley rider but until the Ministry of Transport could be persuaded to close its newest stretch of road we had to do battle via the more traditional trolley races.

I had owned my trolley for simply ages, Dad had helped me make it when I was really quite small. I had collected four wheels from the yard of the local rag and bone man and Dad had them fitted to axels by the welder at his work. One was fitted to the rear of the trolley that was itself constructed out of four floor boards nailed side by side with solid wooden slats. The whole affair tapered at the front to which was fastened the steering bar and the front pair of wheels. We had heated up a poker in the lounge fire until it was red hot then burned holes through the steering bar and nose of the trolley. A heavy coach bolt held it all together and permitted the steering bar to swivel.

Until such time as Jim and I could test our skill in the ultimate M1 race we devised all kinds of minor trials to evaluate the other's ability at trolley driving. There were three ways to drive a trolley: *Belly Down Bum Up* where the rider lay flat along the length of the vehicle placing his hands direct on the front axle bar so causing the least wind resistance. *Look No Hands* was the trickiest way of all, the rider had to sit with his feet on the steering bar, fold his arms across his chest and use only his legs. The third way was to tie a rope to each side of the front axle and steer *Donkey Derby* by pulling the way it was desired to go. Each and every test had to be undertaken using all three methods.

Jim set out five empty bake bean tins in a line along the footpath at the front of the house. The test was to steer one's trolley between each without hitting any. First donkey derby then belly up bum down and finally look no hands. I successful completed the test.

"Now you have to do it in reverse," Jim chuckled.

I doubted if Jim would be able to do it himself, his trolley had big rear wheels that would be certain to clip the tins, but he was the challenger and I the challenged, the rules said I had to go first.

One of my challenges was an adaptation of the emergency stop from the adult driving test. We each fitted brakes to our trollies in the form of a single length of stout wood screwed to the side. When the handle, or top, of the wood was pushed forward that beneath the pivot jammed against the rear wheel stopping the trolley. If you could get enough speed up and rammed the brake on sharply enough it was possible to skid leaving rubber tyre marks on the pavement. The test was to see who make the longest skid marks.

Of course the only real test of skill was speed. We used to drag our trollies up to the top of Sutton Oak Road and the brow of the steepest hill in the district. The road itself was always heavy with traffic but the pavement was normally void of pedestrians. So this became our number one grand prix circuit. Some days I would be the fastest and on others Jim would come first.

There were, of course, other trolley riders besides Jim and I but they were decidedly second division material. Keith, for example, rode such a ramshackled old heap that it was a miracle it went along at all. Steven was posh so never called his trolley a trolley, it was a go-kart. What nonsense, who did he think he was ? Snob ! And then there was Di.

Dad made Di a trolley giving in to his incessant whining over a period of several weeks. It was modelled on my own but a little shorter and not quite so heavy. I tried it out on Sutton Oak Hill but I was far too used to my own machine so did not like it very much. Di's novice skill at driving coupled with the trolley's smaller design would never see him as a threat to the domination of the sport by Jim and myself. With a little care I made two "L" plates out of white card and red crayon, fixing them to the front and back of Di's trolley. He thought it funny but he would then wouldn't he.

It was Jim who decided upon the Great Trolley Race, The Sutton Oak Hill Grand Prix. Racing would be by invitation only, each contestant would pay an entry fee of two shillings with the winner scooping the lot. Of course Jim and I would be there, one of us after all was going to be the winner. Keith was invited, just so there was somebody to come last and Steven with his go-kart making four of us.

"Pity we can't find another driver," Jim observed, "just to get the winnings up to ten bob."

Ten bob ? What I could do with ten bob. It was a small fortune. "There's always Di," I explained. Now whatever made me say that ?

Jim pondered, would it be fair ? Di lacked experience but then his entry fee would make up the winnings. He agreed to the invitation being offered and I was instructed to sign him on. I would do it that evening after tea.

The next job was to decide upon the rules. It wouldn't be possible to race five trollies down the hill at the same time, the pavement wasn't wide enough. What was needed was some kind of time trial. Jim tore a sheet out of his English exercise book and we sat down to work out details. Each trolley rider would race down Sutton Oak Hill three times, once in each of the three approved riding positions. Times would be kept for individual laps then added together against each driver, the one with the lowest figure would be the winner and receive the ten shillings.

"Who's going to keep time ?" I asked.

"It'll have to be someone who's impartial, not one of the five riders I mean."

"It'll have to be someone who can add up as well," I said. "We can't afford any mistakes with so much prize money at stake."

"How about Mickey Turner, he's brilliant at Maths and his Dad's a football referee ?"

"What's a football referee got to do with it ?"

"Football referees have stop watches don't they so he could borrow it and use it to keep time."

"Do you fancy asking Old Man Turner if he'd let us use his best football referee's stop watch to time a trolley race ?"

Mickey didn't either. His dad had a terrible temper and was known as the grumpiest parent at Banners Gate County Primary School. However, Mickey agreed that if we made it worth his while he would sneak it out, do the timing then put it back before his dad was any the wiser.

"What do you mean, make it worth your while ?"

"You pay me half a crown to do the job," Mickey explained.

"Half a crown ! That would mean our prize money would have to be cut to seven and six. What do you think Richard ?"

I already had the answer. "I say we put the entry fee up to two and six from two bob, that'll get Mickey his half-crown."

"Good thinking." So that was organised.

It was at the next day that Mickey came up with a problem. "You can't see the top of the hill from the bottom," he explained, "so I won't be able to time things properly. I won't be able to see the start and set the watch."

"How about standing half way and watching the start and the finish from there ?" I suggested.

"No good, I thought of that," he replied. "In the middle you can't see either the top or the bottom, the hill's too steep."

I suppose you could always ride down with each driver and time them that way," Jim offered.

"What about wind resistance ?" I protested.

"Forget about any wind resistance," Mickey protested, "if you think I'd risk my Old Man's stop watch on fifteen trolley dashes down Sutton Oak Hill you must be off your head. It'd be sure to get busted and he'd knock me into the middle of next week !"

Um, we had a problem right enough and one the best mathematician and the two best trolley riders in the school could not solve.

"If only I'd had that Dan Dare Radio Station for my birthday," Di said when I told him the race looked like being called off."

"But what use would a Dan Dare Radio Station be ?" I have to confess in spite of my interest in interplanetary travel I knew very little about the subject save it being the latest toy designed about the Dan Dare space stories.

"It's got a walkie talkie set in it. If the starter had the base set at the top of the hill he could tell the time keeper on the remote when he set the trolley off."

You know for a fool my brother was quite clever. "But you didn't get a Dan Dare Radio Station for your birthday did you !"

"No, but Simon Turner did and it's his brother Mickey who's going to be the time keeper so he'd be bound to help."

Simon Turner drove a much harder bargain than did his brother. Not only did he want half a crown to use his Dan Dare Radio Station but he also wanted another half a crown for the batteries. So up went the entry fee to three shillings and six pence. Keith and Snobby Steven protested but paid up in the end. To soften the blow it was agreed that the winner, whoever he turned out to be, would buy the other four an ice cream once the race was over. If I won they'd make do with penny ice-pops, none of your sixpenny Mivi's, I wanted as much of the prize money left intact as possible.

The grand prix was set for the Wednesday afternoon of half-term and every one of us went into strict training. We paid our entry fees to Mickey Turner who would act as judge as well as time keeper. I prepared my trolley for the challenge. I oiled the wheels, greased the steering bolt and practised the entire day before the race. When I got to the hill Jim, Keith and Snobby Steven were already there testing modifications on their own vehicles. Only Di didn't seem to be bothered about things but then it was possible that even Keith would beat him so I guess he could see little point in making any effort before the time of the actual event.

Although Di stuffed his face as usual, ever since his teeth had grown he hadn't stopped eating, I didn't eat very much that lunch time. I wanted to be fit and I had this thing about keeping the wind resistance down, I could not afford to put on weight at the last minute. With the washing up out of the way we took up the steering ropes of our trollies and dragged them to the foot of Sutton Oak Hill.

The other drivers were already there as were the Turner Brothers. Mickey had his dad's stop watch and Simon the Radio Station with, I trust, a new set of batteries. Jim had written the names of all the drivers on slips of paper then folded them up. He offered them to Mickey to draw out the race order. Jim, himself, was to go first, then Keith, me third, Snobby Steven fourth and Di last. We agreed it didn't matter which order each driver chose to race the three styles. I had kind of decided to start with look no hands, then donkey derby and to keep belly down and bum up for my last descent of the hill but I would wait and see what the others did.

We walked to the top of the hill pulling the trollies behind us, the Turner Brothers checked the radio link. It crackled, after all it was only a toy or perhaps the batteries needed replacing (I bet he had pocketed that extra half a crown rather than use it on batteries) but it worked well enough. Jim moved to the start line and selected the belly down bum up stance, flattening himself against the wood of his trolley, trying to mould to its shape. The starter began the count down.

"Ready Jim, after five then. Five – four – three – two – one – OFF !"

Jim gave a kick to start the trolley moving then four more as it gathered momentum. We all watched as he sped towards the bottom. It may not have been possible to see the top from the bottom but you could certainly see the bottom from the top. We watched him all the way down.

"Twenty-five point two seconds," Mickey crackled over the Dan Dare Radio Station. Although we had never before timed our races down Sutton Oak Hill we knew it was a pretty good time.

By comparison Keith took an age using the look no hands method.

"Fifty-one seconds dead," Mickey reported.

Me next. I decided to stick with my plan to do the same as Keith with look no hands, I was certain to better his time. I took my place, settled into position making myself as comfortable as possible. I felt a heavy pair of hands on my back to push me off.

"Five – four – three – two – one – OFF !" A fierce shove and down I started.

I began counting in my head, I just had to beat Keith although riding that was I knew I could not overtake Jim's leading time, my chance would come in the final round. Twenty-three, twenty-four, twenty-five, the descent was taking forever, twenty-six, twenty-seven, twenty-eight. How long had Keith taken ? Fifty-one seconds ? I had to beat Keith's time. Twenty-six, twenty-seven, I'd said that before, twenty-seven, twenty-seven. Come on, come on I had to beat Keith. Where was the finish line ? It looked miles away. Come on, come on, come on, come on !

"How long ? How long ?" Once past Mickey I jumped off, grabbed the trolley and screamed again. "Mickey how long ?"

"Forty-nine point three."

"Forty-nine point three, I'd beaten Keith but only just. I'd have to do better in the next round.

I waited at the bottom of the hill to note the times of Steven and Di. Steven used the fast belly down method and achieved a time of thirty-two point seven seconds while Di rode donkey derby and a time of thirty-one point two. So the position after first round was Jim first, Di second. Di second ?, Steven third, me fourth and Keith, as anticipated, last. Even using the slow no hands style I was not pleased with my performance.

At the end of the second round I was still in fourth position, the only satisfaction came from Di slipping back to third place. Jim had lost his lead to Snobby Steven and Keith was still coming in last. For the final round Keith, Di and I were all to ride belly down, Jim was finishing with donkey derby and Steven look no hands, Mickey Turner had added up the total times.

Snobby Steven   67.4 seconds
Jim   75 .0 seconds
Di Central Eating   78.8 seconds
Me   82.5 seconds
Keith   86.4 seconds

I tried to calculate the time I would have to achieve if I was going to win, then I tried to work out what I needed to avoid coming last. I couldn't come last, I should be the winner or at the very, very least runner up. My brain ached with the mathematical calculations but there were too many variable or perhaps it was just that I wasn't good enough at adding up.

So there we were at the top of Sutton Oak Hill shivering with excitement as the final round began. As with the other two races Jim went first. Riding donkey derby he crouched low clutching the steering rope. Every eye watched every inch of the descent then every breath was held as we awaited he official time from Mickey Turner. Thirty-four point seven, that was a slow time for a donkey derby, my own had been thirty-two point six.

"That gives a total race time," Mickey's voice came over the Dan Dare Radio Station, "of one-o-nine point seven."

My time so far was eighty-two point five. I attempted the maths again, which meant I would have to make the belly down run in under twenty-seven point two to beat Jim. That shouldn't be too difficult, Keith made his belly down run in thirty-one point two to give him a grand total of one-one-seven point six. Pathetic ! I was next. Twenty-seven point two, I had to beat twenty-seven point two. My heart thumped and the adrenaline flowed, the butterflies in my stomach developed hiccups. Twenty-seven point two.

"Five – four – three – two – one – OFF !"

I stabbed my foot out and started the run. Six times more I scooted the trolley forward until I felt it had reached its maximum speed. Gripping the steering bar like a vice I pressed my body against the wood until they became as one then set my eyes to focus on the finish line at the bottom. There stood Mickey Turner, watch in hand, counting off the seconds. Twenty-seven point two, I had to make it in under twenty-seven point two. This time I hadn't started counting in my head, I just hoped I was making good enough speed.

The wind blew in my face and I felt it glide over my body, the shirt rippled on my back. Twenty-seven point two, I was sure I was going to make it.

It was all over so quickly, I flashed past Mickey and skidded to a halt some twenty-five yards further on. I didn't get the chance to ask him before he volunteered the information.

"Twenty-eight point nine, Richard." Words of doom, "that gives you a total race time of one eleven point four."

Damn, damn, damn, damn, damn, damn, damn ! I'd missed it. Curses, by one point seven seconds I'd missed it. Jim would win and I would settle for second place. Second place and no ten shilling prize money. I was so fed up I paid little or no attention at all to Snobby Steven's final run. At the end of the second round true enough he was first place but with the final fun in the look no hands position it wasn't possible that he would manage to beat either Jim or myself. I was right, with a time of fifty-one point six he fell right back behind even Keith. Oh well just Di to run down and it would be time for Jim to be confirmed as winner.

Mickey had been right about the camber of the hill. Standing at the bottom it was impossible to see Di start his run although we heard Simon's voice over the Dan Dare hand set say he was on his way. Mickey clicked the watch to start counting, he called the time off every five seconds. He had only just called ten when Di came into view. Like lightening he flashed down the hill. "Fifteen." How he could be so fast on a trolley I could not imagine. I saw his foot reach out and give two quick pushes at the ground, speeding the trolley toward the finish line. "Twenty." Mickey had hardly finished speaking when Di hurtled past us. The watch clicked to a halt.

"Twenty-four point three which gives total of one-o-three point one made makes Di the grand prix winner.

Brother Di the winner ? Not Jim ? Jim pushed into second place by the youngest driver, my brother Di ? Had I really been pushed into third place ? Had Mickey Turner added up the times incorrectly ? No, he produced a sheet of paper with all the times neatly recorded, there was no mistake. Di Central

Eating was the winner of the first Sutton Oak Hill Invitation Grand Prix.

Jim offered his congratulations, as did Keith and Snobby Steven. Reluctantly I joined them. Mickey handed over the prize money and we all followed Di to the ice cream shop. He was generous towards us all, including Mickey and Simon in the round. I don't know what he spent the rest of the prize money on but I don't mind telling you that ice cream nearly choked me.

AND THEN WE WERE THREE:
My Mum used to spend most evenings in front of the television, indeed she still does, clicking together knitting needles. Nearly all of our jumpers came from her hobby which had an output to rival the factories of Marks and Sparks. She gave talks on the subject at the Young Wives Club and, although an amateur, she was an acknowledged local expert. Nobody, therefore, to begin with at least paid very much attention to her increased level of production.

I think I was the first to notice there was something out of place. The strange thing was she started using only white wool and the results of her efforts were far too small to fit either Di or myself. Instead they were stored away in an old blue suitcase on top of Mum and Dad's bedroom wardrobe. It didn't make a lot of sense to me.

Di said something about Mum putting on weight but she was always fussing about going on a diet at the time turning enough food out of her kitchen to feed an army.

Ever since he had been born I had shared a bedroom with Brother Di. He was more than a bit of a pest but I got used to his snoring and nightmares, even his collection of teddy bears which was a source of embarrassment every time a friend came into our room. Besides the box room was so full of collected junk it was quite uninhabitable. Then one Saturday Dad instructed us both to help him clear it all out.

"Why are we doing this Dad ?"

"Better ask your mother."

"But she's not here is she ?"

"Where's she gone ?"

"Just popped out to look at some wallpaper."

"Wallpaper ? What does she want wallpaper for ?"

"To put on walls idiot."

The sudden desire to decorate didn't fit in. Dad had only just finished the lounge and the wallpaper in the bedroom was less than a year old.

"Which room are you going to decorate ?"

"This one."

"Why ?"

"You can't expect the baby to sleep in it as it is now."

BABY ! BABY ! What baby ? The secret was out, Mum was expecting a baby ! Jeeps I didn't want another brother, Di was more than enough ! But then what if was a sister, a sister ? Impossible !

Di has always been naïve, he still is, but this was one area of the subject I have to confess I joined him in. To the best of my knowledge babies came from the shops just like everything else. Not shops like those down the road, Ken Riley Hardware or Tom O'Connell's Greengrocery, but big shops up in the town. The department stores like Lewis's or Rackham's, after all when I had been there with Gran I saw them. They had a big sign on the wall: *Baby Department.*

So the box room was duly decorated with soppy infant wallpaper, Great Aunt Gladys sewed up matching curtains and Gran gave Mum five pounds to buy a new carpet. The cot, pram and baby bath both Di and I had used were unpacked from the attic, dusted down and made ready for the baby's arrival.

It was so humiliating when Mum began remembering when we had been little babies and then telling everyone about it. "I do so wish you'd never grown up," she cooed. Daft !

Was that why she wanted another baby ? When that one started to grow up would she want another, and then another ? Where would it end ? How much did babies cost ? Babies from Lewis's would be cheaper than those from Rackham's, Rackham's was where the posh people shopped. I ventured to suggest this to a friend at school who explained that babies were delivered to homes by birds called storks. It was so unlikely I knew he was making it all up.

My little sister, yes it was a girl, was a long time coming. I presume they must have been out of stock at Lewis's. She eventually came along one cold March day. Mum took to her bed and Gran came round to look after us, Neither Di nor I, not even Dad were allowed up there to see her. Later on a lady called the midwife came round. She had with her a big black bag in which I presume she had the baby. She must have been up to town, to Lewis's to collect it. Babies where back in stock and on the shelves.

When I first saw it, it was bawling its little head off, it was making more noise than even Di could on a good day. I wondered if Lewis's gave refunds but then Mum looked happy so I thought it would not have been fair to send it back.

It was named Anne after the young Princess Anne. Thank goodness Mum and Dad were not that patriotic when I was born, I would hate to have been called Charles.

Pictures of Prince Charles and Princess Anne appeared on special saving stamps which were on sale each week at school. Charles's stamps cost half a crown and were blue in colour while Anne's were green and cost just one shilling. Di and I used to be sent to school with a shilling every Friday to buy one of Princess Anne's saving stamps which we suck in a special book. When the book was full we would take it down to the post office and exchange it for a savings certificate which was paced in a bank book. Years later we cashed them in and transferred the money to an organisation called Barclays but that's another story.

"I hope she don't grow up to look like those saving stamps," Di observed, "'cos she's dead ugly." True the picture of Princess Anne was hardly flattering but he should learn to keep his mouth shut. People have ended up in The Tower of London for saying less.

"Your new sister in every way is a princess in her own right," Gran said but neither of us knew what she meant by that. Perhaps she'd marry Prince Charles.

Dad leaned over and kissed his new daughter, then he kissed Mum. "Well done darling, she's perfect." What did he mean, well done ? Mum hadn't done very much. After all it was the midwife that had been up town to buy her, all Mum had done was to stay in bed.

If Di was the perfect pest of brother then Anne was double so as a sister and yet I loved her so very much. When Mum first let me hold her I went all tingly and the hair stood up on the back of my neck. The smell of talcum powder and baby cream was sweet even if Di said it stank. I'm not quite sure if I could say I loved her so much when she exercised her lungs in the middle of the night but as she grew up Anne and I became very close indeed. As I had done before her, she found pronouncing David almost impossible. Just as well we called him Di. But it was simply ages before she could manage Central Eating.

THE GYPSY'S CURSE:
NOW HANG ON A MINUTE !

Just stop right there will you ! This is David Albon writing now, not that fool of a brother of mine who thinks he is the next Enid Blyton or Roald Dhal. What's this all about – Wild Adventures ? Fish and platinum plated pitchforks ? You don't honestly believe all that rubbish do you ?

Do you ?

Pardon, what did you say ?

I thought so !

Now let's be realistic shall we. Brother Richard may be one of the most prolific writers of his time but nobody ever reads any of it. I know he's got dreams of fame and fortune but William Shakespeare he is not. Let's face it he hasn't ever had so much as a full stop published. But, just in case, just in case someone is fool enough to pick up the manuscript and have nothing better to do than read it I would like to set the record straight.

My name is David Albon, yes OK then Di Central Eating if you like but nobody's called me that for years. If Richard doesn't watch out I'll tell you what we used to call him. What the heck why not, you'd like to know wouldn't you ? *Dickie-Dirt,* that's what we used to call him. Dickie-Dirt ! Dickie because it's short for Richard and Dirt, well that was my Mother's idea. Richard, you see, was allergic to water, at least when it was mixed with soap. He certainly was a scruffy kid, I wish some of his posh friends of today could have seen him then.

Dickie-Dirt, what a cheek to sit down and here expose all my childhood secrets. I'll get him, you want and see if I don't, I'll stitch him up. So what can I tell you about him ? What dark secrets can I reveal ? There was the grasshopper hopper he put in Mum's teapot and the time he baked a cake for the school hobbies exhibition, the teacher who judged the competition was taken into hospital with food poisoning. Then there was the time when he got drunk on Dad's home brew and slept it off in the garden shed before anyone found out. There you are Mum and Dad, you never knew about that did you ?

Well if daft Brother Dickie-Dirt can tell you about my dreams of being a pop star or making pretend voyages into space then I can tell you about the gypsy's curse. So sit down, pin back your lug holes and cop a load of this !

To this very day Brother Richard, sorry I mean Dickie-Dirt, has a phobia about frogs. Yes, those little jumpy things you find at the edges of ponds. It's not that he doesn't like them or is even scared of them, more accurately he is terrified. At the very sight he becomes physically sick and his whole body turns to a quivering wreck. He once applied for a job with MI5 but was turned down on account of this fear. It seemed they thought all the enemy would have to do would be to wave a frog under his nose for Dickie to reveal every state secret ever known to mankind. Last summer he found a frog in his garden, it wasn't doing very much just sitting there sunning itself but it sent him into cardiac arrest. His two sons had to go and catch it, put it in a dustbin bag and then his wife had to drive it ten miles away and release it. he refused to go back into the garden for nearly a week and cancelled a barbecue he was hosting for ten business customers. All because of the gypsy's curse.

I don't remember how old we were at the time but it must have been before Dad contracted the Percy Thrower bug for our garden was something of a jungle. Dickie and I were playing in the undergrowth pretending to be Tarzan or something similar. It wasn't much of a game, Dickie always wanted to direct the play never letting me be the hero and never playing the way I wanted to. It was some time during the school holidays because we had been playing all morning and intended to continue after lunch. Mum was in the kitchen cooking, Mum was always in the kitchen cooking, and Dad was out at work. It was before Anne invaded our lives, did you read what he wrote about her ? Where she came from I mean – Lewis's Baby Department ! I ask you, what a prize pellock ! Anyway, there we were stalking some ferocious beast. Armed with poison tipped spears we were set on sending it to the hereafter so saving all the surrounding native villages from its nightly reign of terror. No more would the people fear their children being carried off, no longer would the shepherd lose his flock to the foul beast that came with the darkness.

We were slashing our way through the undergrowth when the foul beast jumped right in front of Dickie. It threw itself at him, slapping its body against his lower leg. Fearless Tarzan flung down his spear and bolted for the safety of the house.

"Mummy, Mummy there's a frog in the garden !"

I did not follow him immediately but instead continued to stalk the creature, I had other plans. It was easy to track him down and easy to capture him. I held the evil brute of the forest in my two hands and followed Dickie into the house.

Mum had left the kitchen and was at the front door talking to a gypsy woman who was trying to sell lace table covers and wooden clothes pegs. You don't see that sort of thing these days, Romanies are more interested in scrap cars and other metals, but when we were children it was quite common for their women folk to peddle their wares door to door. Mum was just wondering if one of the lace table covers would make a suitable birthday present for Great Aunt Gladys when Dickie burst in, still shouting he clutched at Mother's skirts.

"Mummy, mummy there's a frog in the garden," he continued to blurt, "it jumped right at me." The shock has quite un-nerved him.

Mum was obviously quite embarrassed. "Don't be so silly Richard, stop all that noise, besides it's gone now."

"No it aint Mum," I made my entrance, "I caught it and here it is." I offered it up for Dickie to look at. He screeched hiding behind Mum's back.

"Di take it away," she ordered. "Put it back in the garden." I tossed it out the front door past the gypsy woman where it landed on the path and sat there.

"Make it go away Mummy, please make it go away," Dickie pleaded.

Bravely I went outside, put my toe behind it and helped it on its way. The animal hopped off into the road. Just then a car came past and splattered it. To a seven year old it was lovely, guts spewed all over the tarmac. At nine years of age, however, Dickie did not appreciate it and continued his hysterical screaming.

"I'm so sorry about all this," Mum apologised, "please don't go away I want to buy one of those lovely lace covers. I'll just get my purse."

"No hurry Dearie," the old woman smiled, "and don't worry. Come here my little man, let the old gypsy lady take away your troubles."

Dickie didn't know if he was more scared of a gypsy than he was of the frog but fear is a great motivator, terror is even better. He did as he was told as Mum pushed him off her to go and find her purse. The gypsy woman smiled. "He can't hurt you now, his body's dead and the spirit of animals never hurt anyone. What makes you so frightened ?"

"It was horrible," Dickie sobbed, "all jumpy and nasty."

"There, there," she soothed, "he didn't mean to frighten you and now the poor little thing is dead."

"But it was horrible."

"I know. What's your name ?"

"Richard."

"Well Richard let the old gypsy lady weave a little magic for you." She placed a hand on Richard's head and closed her eyes.

"There all better now. You'll never lose your fear of frogs Richard but the spirit of this dead frog will watch over you and protect you for the rest of your life."

Mum bought her lace table cloth and the gypsy woman was gone. Before she left she kissed Dickie gently on the cheek. "Now remember what I have said to you Richard."

All mumbo jumbo if you ask me but the fact remains to this day Brother Richard has a nauseating terror of frogs. Their very sight illogically makes him want to vomit from every inch of his body and yet in all other ways he has been terribly lucky in everything he attempts. I wasn't exactly telling the truth earlier about MI5, all his working life Dickie has run his own business which is fabulously successful. He has a lovely wife, three super kids and all in all he's not a bag guy even if he is my big brother. Perhaps there was something in the gypsy's spell after all, or was it a curse ? Spell for fortune, curse for frogs. I expect the old girl's long dead by now, is her gypsy spirit up there with that of the splattered frog, looking down on all he does and guiding his destiny ? I'm going to put it to the test.

In between business deals Brother Richard likes to write books. This is his ninth full-length novel. I've hacked into his word processor and pulled out copies of them all. He's never attempted to sell any to a publisher, I guess he's got enough intelligence to realise no sane person would ever want to read any such illiterate scribble. To the end of this manuscript I have now added my own final chapter and fully intend to send copies to a variety of publishing houses. With a certainty each and every one of them will dismiss the opus, so proving the gypsy's spell to be nothing more than a load of baloney. If, however, one takes sufficient leave of its senses to print and distribute such nonsense, if you are reading these words in a small book complete with glossy cover, author's pseudonym, line drawings and ISBN, perhaps purchased from W H Smith's then you will know the gypsy's spell to be true and we'll say no more. Good Bye !

POST SCRIPT:
Well there you go, three stories from me to you. What did you think ?

That was good, perhaps I could write something a bit like that myself.

OR:

What a load of old rubbish ! I could do better myself.

Either was pick up your pen, or perhaps your laptop, and start writing. Write **3Stories4Me.**

Max Robinson aka David

Printed in Great Britain
by Amazon

52516389R00096